Fair fall the lights, the harbour lights
That brought me in to thee
And peace drop down on that low roof
For the sight that I did see
And the voice my dear that rang so clear
All for the love of me.
For O, for O with brows bent low
By the flickering candle's gleam
Her wedding gown it was she wrought
Sewing the long white seam

[*The Long White Seam.—Page* 89.]

BOSTON:
ROBERTS BROTHERS.
1871.

THE

MONITIONS OF THE UNSEEN,

AND

Poems of Love and Childhood.

BY JEAN INGELOW.

AUTHOR'S EDITION.

BOSTON:
ROBERTS BROTHERS.
1871.

CAMBRIDGE:
PRESS OF JOHN WILSON AND SON.

CONTENTS.

	PAGE
The Monitions of the Unseen	1
A Birthday Walk	33
Not in vain I waited	37
A Gleaning Song	39
With a Diamond	41
Fancy	42
Compensation	43
Looking Down	44
Married Lovers	45
A Winter Song	49
Binding Sheaves	52
Work	54
Wishing	55
To ——	56
On the Borders of Cannock Chase	57
The Mariner's Cave	58
A Reverie	76
Defton Wood	79
The Snowdrop Monument (in Lichfield Cathedral)	81
An Ancient Chess-King dug from some Ruins	86

PAGE
Comfort in the Night 87
Though all Great Deeds 88
The Long White Seam 89
An Old Wife's Song 91
Cold and Quiet 95
A Snow Mountain 97
Sleep (a Woman speaks) 98
Promising (a Man speaks) 99
Love 100
Poems on the Deaths of Three Lovely Children . 101

The Two Margarets.
I. Margaret by the Mere Side 121
II. Margaret in the Xebec 140

THE MONITIONS OF THE UNSEEN.

THERE are who give themselves to work for men,—
To raise the lost, to gather orphaned babes
And teach them, pitying of their mean estate,
To feel for misery, and to look on crime
With ruth, till they forget that they themselves
Are of the race, themselves among the crowd
Under the sentence and outside the gate,
And of the family and in the doom.
Cold is the world; they feel how cold it is,
And wish that they could warm it. Hard is life
For some. They would that they could soften it;
And, in the doing of their work, they sigh
As if it was their choice and not their lot;
And, in the raising of their prayer to God,
They crave his kindness for the world he made,

Till they, at last, forget that he, not they,
Is the true lover of man.

Now, in an ancient town, that had sunk low, —
Trade having drifted from it, while there stayed
Too many, that it erst had fed, behind, —
There walked a curate once, at early day.

It was the summer-time; but summer air
Came never, in its sweetness, down that dark
And crowded alley, — never reached the door
Whereat he stopped, — the sordid, shattered door.

He paused, and, looking right and left, beheld
Dirt and decay, the lowering tenements
That leaned toward each other; broken panes
Bulging with rags, and grim with old neglect;
And reeking hills of formless refuse, heaped
To fade and fester in a stagnant air.

But he thought nothing of it: he had learned
To take all wretchedness for granted, — he,
Reared in a stainless home, and radiant yet
With the clear hues of healthful English youth,
Had learned to kneel by beds forlorn, and stoop
Under foul lintels. He could touch, with hand
Unshrinking, fevered fingers; he could hear
The language of the lost, in haunt and den, —
So dismal, that the coldest passer-by
Must needs be sorry for them, and, albeit
They cursed, would dare to speak no harder words
Than these, — "God help them!"

Ay! a learned man
The curate in all woes that plague mankind, —
Too learned, for he was but young. His heart
Had yearned till it was overstrained, and now
He — plunged into a narrow slough unblest,
Had struggled with its deadly waters, till
His own head had gone under, and he took

Small joy in work he could not look to aid
Its cleansing.
Yet, by one right tender tie,
Hope held him yet. The fathers coarse and dull,
Vile mothers hard, and boys and girls profane,
His soul drew back from. He had worked for them, —
Work without joy: but, in his heart of hearts,
He loved the little children; and, whene'er
He heard their prattle innocent, and heard
Their tender voices lisping sacred words
That he had taught them, — in the cleanly calm
Of decent school, by decent matron held, —
Then would he say, "I shall have pleasure yet,
In these."
But now, when he pushed back that door
And mounted up a flight of ruined stairs,
He said not that. He said, "Oh! once I thought
The little children would make bright for me
The crown they wear who have won many souls
For righteousness; but oh, this evil place!

Hard lines it gives them, cold and dirt abhorred, —
Hunger and nakedness, in lieu of love,
And blows instead of care.
                                        And so they die,
The little children that I love, — they die, —
They turn their wistful faces to the wall,
And slip away to God."
                                        With that, his hand
He laid upon a latch and lifted it,
Looked in full quietly, and entered straight.

What saw he there? He saw a three-years child,
That lay a-dying on a wisp of straw
Swept up into a corner. O'er its brow
The damps of death were gathering: all alone,
Uncared for, save that by its side was set
A cup, it waited. And the eyes had ceased
To look on things at hand. He thought they gazed
In wistful wonder, or some faint surmise
Of coming change, — as though they saw the gate

Of that fair land that seems to most of us
Very far off.
When he beheld the look,
He said, "I knew, I knew how this would be!
Another! Ay, and but for drunken blows
And dull forgetfulness of infant need,
This little one had lived." And thereupon
The misery of it wrought upon him so,
That, unaware, he wept. Oh! then it was
That, in the bending of his manly head,
It came betwen the child and that whereon
He gazed, and, when the curate glanced again,
Those dying eyes, drawn back to earth once more,
Looked up into his own, and smiled.
He drew
More near, and kneeled beside the small frail thing,
Because the lips were moving; and it raised
Its baby hand, and stroked away his tears,
And whispered, "Master! master!" and so died.

Now, in that town there was an ancient church,
A minster of old days which these had turned
To parish uses: there the curate served.
It stood within a quiet swarded Close,
Sunny and still, and, though it was not far
From those dark courts where poor humanity
Struggled and swarmed, it seemed to wear its own
Still atmosphere about it, and to hold
That old-world calm within its precincts pure
And that grave rest which modern life foregoes.

When the sad curate, rising from his knees,
Looked from the dead to heaven, — as, unaware,
Men do when they would track departed life, —
He heard the deep tone of the minster-bell
Sounding for service, and he turned away
So heavy at heart, that, when he left behind
That dismal habitation, and came out
In the clear sunshine of the minster-yard,
He never marked it. Up the aisle he moved,

With his own gloom about him; then came forth,
And read before the folk grand words and calm, —
Words full of hope; but into his dull heart
Hope came not. As one talketh in a dream,
And doth not mark the sense of his own words,
He read; and, as one walketh in a dream,
He after walked toward the vestment-room,
And never marked the way he went by, — no,
Nor the gray verger that before him stood,
The great church-keys depending from his hand,
Ready to follow him out and lock the door.

At length, aroused to present things, but not
Content to break the sequence of his thought,
Nor ready for the working day that held
Its busy course without, he said, "Good friend,
Leave me the keys: I would remain awhile."
And, when the verger gave, he moved with him
Toward the door distraught, then shut him out,
And locked himself within the church alone.

The minster-church was like a great brown cave,
Fluted and fine with pillars, and all dim
With glorious gloom; but, as the curate turned,
Suddenly shone the sun, — and roof and walls,
Also the clustering shafts from end to end,
Were thickly sown all over, as it were,
With seedling rainbows. And it went and came
And went, that sunny beam, and drifted up
Ethereal bloom to flush the open wings
And carven cheeks of dimpled cherubim,
And dropped upon the curate as he passed,
And covered his white raiment and his hair.

Then did look down upon him from their place,
High in the upper lights, grave mitred priests,
And grand old monarchs in their flowered gowns
And capes of miniver; and therewithal
(A veiling cloud gone by) the naked sun
Smote with his burning splendor all the pile,
And in there rushed, through half-translucent panes,

Among the branches of the tree of life —
Through all the ordered forest of the shafts,
Shooting on high to enter into light,
That swam aloft, — he took his silent way,
And in the southern transept sat him down,
Covered his face, and thought.
He said, "No pain,
No passion, and no aching, heart o' mine,
Doth stir within thee. Oh! I would there did:
Thou art so dull, so tired. I have lost
I know not what. I see the heavens as lead:
They tend no whither. Ah! the world is bared
Of her enchantment now: she is but earth
And water. And, though much hath passed away,
There may be more to go. I may forget
The joy and fear that have been: there may live
No more for me the fervency of hope
Nor the arrest of wonder.
"Once I said,
Content will wait on work, though work appear

Unfruitful.' Now I say, 'Where is the good?
What is the good?' A lamp when it is lit
Must needs give light; but I am like a man
Holding his lamp in some deserted place
Where no foot passeth. Must I trim my lamp,
And ever painfully toil to keep it bright,
When use for it is none? I must; I will.
Though God withhold my wages, I must work,
And watch the bringing of my work to nought, —
Weed in the vineyard through the heat o' the day,
And, overtasked, behold the weedy place
Grow ranker yet in spite of me.

"Oh! yet
My meditated words are trodden down
Like a little wayside grass. Castaway shells,
Lifted and tossed aside by a plunging wave,
Have no more force against it than have I
Against the sweeping, weltering wave of life,
That, lifting and dislodging me, drives on,
And notes not mine endeavor."

Afterward,
He added more words like to these; to wit,
That it was hard to see the world so sad:
He would that it were happier. It was hard
To see the blameless overborne; and hard
To know that God, who loves the world, should yet
Let it lie down in sorrow, when a smile
From him would make it laugh and sing, — a word
From him transform it to a heaven. He said,
Moreover, "When will this be done? My life
Hath not yet reached the noon, and I am tired;
And oh! it may be that, uncomforted
By foolish hope of doing good and vain
Conceit of being useful, I may live,
And it may be my duty to go on
Working for years and years, for years and years."

But, while the words were uttered, in his heart
There dawned a vague alarm. He was aware
That somewhat touched him, and he lifted up

His face. "I am alone," the curate said, —
"I think I am alone. What is it, then?
I am ashamed! My raiment is not clean.
My lips, — I am afraid they are not clean.
My heart is darkened and unclean. Ah me,
To be a man, and yet to tremble so!
Strange, strange!"
And there was sitting at his feet —
He could not see it plainly — at his feet
A very little child. And, while the blood
Drave to his heart, he set his eye on it,
Gazing, and, lo! the loveliness from heaven
Took clearer form and color. He beheld
The strange, wise sweetness of a dimpled mouth, —
The deep serene of eyes at home with bliss,
And perfect in possession. So it spoke,
"My master!" but he answered not a word;
And it went on: "I had a name, a name.
He knew my name; but here they can forget."
The curate answered: "Nay, I know thee well.

I love thee. Wherefore art thou come?" It said,
"They sent me;" and he faltered, "Fold thy hand,
O most dear little one! for on it gleams
A gem that is so bright I cannot look
Thereon." It said, "When I did leave this world,
That was a tear. But that was long ago;
For I have lived among the happy folk,
You wot of, ages, ages." Then said he,
"Do they forget us, while beneath the palms
They take their infinite leisure?" And, with eyes
That seemed to muse upon him, looking up
In peace the little child made answer, "Nay;"
And murmured, in the language that he loved,
"How is it that his hair is not yet white;
For I and all the others have been long
Waiting for him to come."

"And was it long?"
The curate answered, pondering. "Time being done,
Shall life indeed expand, and give the sense,
In our to-come, of infinite extension?"

Then said the child, "In heaven we children talk
Of the great matters, and our lips are wise;
But here I can but talk with thee in words
That here I knew." And therewithal, arisen,
It said, "I pray you take me in your arms."
Then, being afraid but willing, so he did;
And partly drew about the radiant child,
For better covering its dread purity,
The foldings of his gown. And he beheld
Its beauty, and the tremulous woven light
That hung upon its hair; withal, the robe,
'Whiter than fuller of this world can white,'
That clothed its immortality. And so
The trembling came again, and he was dumb,
Repenting his uncleanness: and he lift
His eyes, and all the holy place was full
Of living things; and some were faint and dim,
As if they bore an intermittent life,
Waxing and waning; and they had no form,
But drifted on like slowly trailèd clouds,

Or moving spots of darkness, with an eye
Apiece. And some, in guise of evil birds,
Came by in troops, and stretched their naked necks,
And some were men-like, but their heads hung down;
And he said, "O my God! let me find grace
Not to behold their faces, for I know
They must be wicked and right terrible."
But while he prayed, lo! whispers; and there moved
Two shadows on the wall. He could not see
The forms of them that cast them: he could see
Only the shadows as of two that sat
Upon the floor, where, clad in women's weeds,
They lisped together. And he shuddered much:
There was a rustling near him, and he feared
Lest they should touch him, and he feel their touch.

"It is not great," quoth one, "the work achieved.
We do, and we delight to do, our best:
But that is little; for, my dear," quoth she,
"This tower and town have been infested long

With angels." — "Ay," the other made reply,
"I had a little evil-one, of late,
That I picked up as it was crawling out
O' the pit, and took and cherished in my breast.
It would divine for me, and oft would moan,
'Pray thee, no churches,' and it spake of this.
But I was harried once, — thou know'st by whom, —
And fled in here; and, when he followed me,
I crouching by this pillar, he let down
His hand, — being all too proud to send his eyes
In its wake, — and, plucking forth my tender imp,
Flung it behind him. It went yelping forth;
And, as for me, I never saw it more.
Much is against us, — very much: the times
Are hard." She paused: her fellow took the word,
Plaining on such as preach and them that plead.
"Even such as haunt the yawning mouths of hell,"
Quoth she, "and pluck them back that run thereto."
Then, like a sudden blow, there fell on him
The utterance of his name. "There is no soul

That I loathe more, and oftener curse. Woe's me,
That cursing should be vain! Ay, he will go
Gather the sucking children, that are yet
Too young for us, and watch and shelter them
Till the strong Angels — pitiless and stern,
But to them loving ever — sweep them in,
By armsful, to the unapproachable fold.

"We strew his path with gold: it will not lie.
'Deal softly with him,' was the master's word.
We brought him all delights: his angel came
And stood between them and his eyes. They spend
Much pains upon him, — keep him poor and low
And unbeloved; and thus he gives his mind
To fill the fateful, the impregnable
Child-fold, and sow on earth the seed of stars.

"Oh! hard is serving against love, — the love
Of the Unspeakable; for if we soil
The souls He openeth out a washing-place;

And if we grudge, and snatch away the bread,
Then will He save by poverty, and gain
By early giving up of blameless life;
And if we shed out gold, He even will save
In spite of gold, — of twice-refinèd gold."

With that the curate set his daunted eyes
To look upon the shadows of the fiends.
He was made sure they could not see the child
That nestled in his arms; he also knew
They were unconscious that his mortal ears
Had new intelligence, which gave their speech
Possible entrance through his garb of clay.

He was afraid, yet awful gladness reached
His soul: the testimony of the lost
Upbraided him; but while he trembled yet,
The heavenly child had lifted up its head
And left his arms, and on the marble floor
Stood beckoning.

And, its touch withdrawn, the place
Was silent, empty; all that swarming tribe
Of evil ones concealed behind the veil,
And shut into their separate world, were closed
From his observance. He arose, and paced
After the little child, — as half in fear
That it would leave him, — till they reached a door;
And then said he, — but much distraught he spoke,
Laying his hand across the lock, — "This door
Shuts in the stairs whereby men mount the tower.
Wouldst thou go up, and so withdraw to heaven?"
It answered, "I will mount them." Then said he,
"And I will follow." — "So thou shalt do well,"
The radiant thing replied, and it went up,
And he, amazed, went after; for the stairs,
Otherwhile dark, were lightened by the rays
Shed out of raiment woven in high heaven,
And hair whereon had smiled the light of God.

With that, they, pacing on, came out at last

Into a dim, weird place, — a chamber formed
Betwixt the roofs: for you shall know that all
The vaulting of the nave, fretted and fine,
Was covered with the dust of ages, laid
Thick with those chips of stone which they had left
Who wrought it; but a high-pitched roof was reared
Above it, and the western gable pierced
With three long narrow lights. Great tie-beams loomed
Across, and many daws frequented there,
The starling and the sparrow littered it
With straw, and peeped from many a shady nook;
And there was lifting up of wings, and there
Was hasty exit when the curate came.
But sitting on a beam and moving not
For him, he saw two fair gray turtle-doves
Bowing their heads, and cooing; and the child
Put forth a hand to touch his own, but straight
He, startled, drew it back, because, forsooth,
A stirring fancy smote him, and he thought
That language trembled on their innocent tongues,
And floated forth in speech that man could hear.

Then said the child, "Yet touch, my master dear."
And he let down his hand, and touched again;
And so it was. "But if they had their way,"
One turtle cooed, "how should this world go on?"

Then he looked well upon them, as he stood
Upright before them. They were feathered doves,
And sitting close together; and their eyes
Were rounded with the rim that marks their kind.
Their tender crimson feet did pat the beam, —
No phantoms they; and soon the fellow-dove
Made answer, "Nay, they count themselves so wise,
There is no task they shall be set to do
But they will ask God why. What mean they so?
The glory is not in the task, but in
The doing it for Him. What should he think,
Brother, this man that must, forsooth, be set
Such noble work, and suffered to behold
Its fruit, if he knew more of us and ours?"

With that the other leaned, as if attent:
"I am not perfect, brother, in his thought."
The mystic bird replied, "Brother, he saith,
'But it is nought: the work is overhard.'
Whose fault is that? God sets not overwork.
He saith the world is sorrowful, and he
Is therefore sorrowful. He cannot set
The crooked straight; — but who demands of him,
O brother, that he should? What! thinks he, then,
His work is God's advantage, and his will
More bent to aid the world than its dread Lord's.
Nay, yet there live amongst us legions fair,
Millions on millions, who could do right well
What he must fail in; and 'twas whispered me,
That chiefly for himself the task is given, —
His little daily task." With that he paused.

Then said the other, preening its fair wing,
"Men have discovered all God's islands now,
And given them names; whereof they are as proud,

And deem themselves as great, as if their hands
Had made them. Strange is man, and strange his pride.
Now, as for us, it matters not to learn
What and from whence we be: How should we tell?
Our world is undiscovered in these skies,
Our names not whispered. Yet, for us and ours,
What joy it is, — permission to come down,
Not souls, as he, to the bosom of their God,
To guide, but to their goal the wingèd fowls,
His lovely lower-fashioned lives to help
To take their forms by legions, fly, and draw
With us the sweet, obedient, flocking things
That ever hear our message reverently,
And follow us far. How should they know their way,
Forsooth, alone? Men say they fly alone;
Yet some have set on record, and averred,
That they, among the flocks, had duly marked
A leader."

Then his fellow made reply:
"They might divine the Maker's heart. Come forth,

Fair dove, to find the flocks, and guide their wings,
For Him that loveth them."
With that, the child
Withdrew his hand, and all their speech was done.
He moved toward them, but they fluttered forth
And fled into the sunshine.
"I would fain,"
Said he, "have heard some more. And wilt thou go?"
He added to the child, for this had turned.
"Ay," quoth he, gently, "to the beggar's place;
For I would see the beggar in the porch."

So they went down together to the door,
Which, when the curate opened, lo! without
The beggar sat; and he saluted him:
"Good morrow, master." "Wherefore art thou here?"
The curate asked: "it is not service-time,
And none will enter now to give thee alms."
Then said the beggar, "I have hope at heart
That I shall go to my poor house no more."

"Art thou so sick that thou dost think to die?"
The curate said. With that the beggar laughed,
And under his dim eyelids gathered tears,
And he was all a-tremble with a strange
And moving exaltation. "Ay," quoth he,
And set his face toward high heaven: "I think
The blessing that I wait on must be near."
Then said the curate, "God be good to thee."
And, straight, the little child put forth his hand,
And touched him. "Master, master, hush!
You should not, master, speak so carelessly
In this great presence."

But the touch so wrought,
That, lo! the dazzled curate staggered back,
For dread effulgence from the beggar's eyes
Smote him, and from the crippled limbs shot forth
Terrible lights, as pure long blades of fire.
"Withdraw thy touch! withdraw thy touch!" he cried,
"Or else shall I be blinded." Then the child
Stood back from him; and he sat down apart,

Recovering of his manhood: and he heard
The beggar and the child discourse of things
Dreadful for glory, till his spirits came
Anew; and, when the beggar looked on him,
He said, "If I offend not, pray you tell
Who and what are you — I behold a face
Marred with old age, sickness, and poverty, —
A cripple with a staff, who long hath sat
Begging, and oftimes moaning, in the porch,
For pain and for the wind's inclemency.
What are you?" Then the beggar made reply,
"I was a delegate, a living power;
My work was bliss, for seeds were in my hand
To plant a new-made world. O happy work!
It grew and blossomed; but my dwelling-place
Was far remote from heaven. I have not seen;
I knew no wish to enter there. But, lo!
There went forth rumors, running out like rays,
How some, that were of power like even to mine,
Had made request to come and find a place

Within its walls. And these were satisfied
With promises, and sent to this far world
To take the weeds of your mortality,
And minister, and suffer grief and pain,
And die like men. Then were they gathered in.
They saw a face, and were accounted kin
To Whom thou knowest, for he is kin to men.

"Then I did wait; and oft, at work, I sang,
'To minister! oh, joy, to minister!'
And, it being known, a message came to me:
'Whether is best, thou forest-planter wise,
To minister to others, or that they
Should minister to thee?' Then, on my face
Low lying, I made answer: 'It is best,
Most High, to minister;' and thus came back
The answer, — 'Choose not for thyself the best:
Go down, and, lo! my poor shall minister,
Out of their poverty, to thee; shall learn
Compassion by thy frailty; and shall oft
Turn back, when speeding home from work, to help

Thee, weak and crippled, home. My little ones,
Thou shalt importune for their slender mite,
And pray, and move them that they give it up
For love of Me.' "
The curate answered him,
"Art thou content, O great one from afar!
If I may ask, and not offend?" He said,
"I am. Behold! I stand not all alone,
That I should think to do a perfect work.
I may not wish to give; for I have heard
'Tis best for me that I receive. For me.
God is the only giver, and His gift
Is one." With that, the little child sighed out,
"O master! master! I am out of heaven
Since noonday, and I hear them calling me.
If you be ready, great one, let us go: —
Hark! hark! they call."
Then did the beggar lift
His face to heaven, and utter forth a cry
As of the pangs of death, and every tree
Moved as if shaken by a sudden wind.

He cried again, and there came forth a hand
From some invisible form, which, being laid
A little moment on the curate's eyes,
It dazzled him with light that brake from it,
So that he saw no more.
"What shall I do?"
The curate murmured, when he came again
To himself and looked about him. "This is strange!
My thoughts are all astray; and yet, methinks,
A weight is taken from my heart. Lo! lo!
There lieth at my feet, frail, white, and dead,
The sometime beggar. He is happy now.
There was a child; but he is gone, and he
Is also happy. I am glad to think
I am not bound to make the wrong go right;
But only to discover, and to do
With cheerful heart, the work that God appoints."

With that, he did compose, with reverent care,
The dead; continuing, "I will trust in Him,
THAT HE CAN HOLD HIS OWN; and I will take

His will, above the work He sendeth me,
To be my chiefest good."
Then went he forth,
"I shall die early," thinking: "I am warned,
By this fair vision, that I have not long
To live." Yet he lived on to good old age;—
Ay, he lives yet, and he is working still.

It may be there are many in like case:
They give themselves, and are in misery
Because the gift is small, and doth not make
The world by so much better as they fain
Would have it. 'Tis a fault; but, as for us,
Let us not blame them. Maybe, 'tis a fault
More kindly looked on by The Majesty
Than our best virtues are. Why, what are we!
What have we given, and what have we desired
To give, the world?
There must be something wrong.
Look to it: let us mend our ways. Farewell.

In sloping fields on narrow plains,
The sheep were feeding on their knees,
As we went through the winding lanes,
Strewed with red buds of alder trees.

A BIRTHDAY WALK.

(WRITTEN FOR A FRIEND'S BIRTHDAY.)

"The days of our life are threescore years and ten."

A BIRTHDAY: — and now a day that rose
With much of hope, with meaning rife —
A thoughtful day from dawn to close:
The middle day of human life.

In sloping fields on narrow plains,
The sheep were feeding on their knees,
As we went through the winding lanes,
Strewed with red buds of alder-trees.

So warm the day — its influence lent
  To flagging thought a stronger wing;
So utterly was winter spent,
  So sudden was the birth of spring.

Wild crocus flowers in copse and hedge —
  In sunlight, clustering thick below,
Sighed for the firwood's shaded ledge,
  Where sparkled yet a line of snow.

And crowded snowdrops faintly hung
  Their fair heads lower for the heat,
While in still air all branches flung
  Their shadowy doubles at our feet.

And through the hedge the sunbeams crept,
  Dropped through the maple and the birch;
And lost in airy distance slept
  On the broad tower of Tamworth Church.

Then, lingering on the downward way,
A little space we resting stood,
To watch the golden haze that lay
Adown that river by the wood.

A distance vague, the bloom of sleep
The constant sun had lent the scene,
A veiling charm on dingles deep
Lay soft those pastoral hills between.

There are some days that die not out,
Nor alter by reflection's power,
Whose converse calm, whose words devout,
For ever rest, the spirit's dower.

And they are days when drops a veil —
A mist upon the distance past;
And while we say to peace — "All hail!"
We hope that always it shall last.

Times when the troubles of the heart
  Are hushed — as winds were hushed that day —
And budding hopes begin to start,
  Like those green hedgerows on our way:

When all within and all around,
  Like hues on that sweet landscape blend,
And Nature's hand has made to sound
  The heartstrings that her touch attend :

When there are rays within, like those
  That streamed through maple and through birch,
And rested in such calm repose
  On the broad tower of Tamworth Church.

NOT IN VAIN I WAITED.

SHE was but a child, a child,
  And I a man grown;
Sweet she was, and fresh, and wild,
  And, I thought, my own.
What could I do? The long grass groweth,
  The long wave floweth with a murmur on:
The why and the wherefore of it all who knoweth?
  Ere I thought to lose her she was grown — and gone.
This day or that day in warm spring weather,
The lamb that was tame will yearn to break its tether.
"But if the world wound thee," I said, "come back to me,
Down in the dell wishing — wishing, wishing for thee."

The dews hang on the white may,
Like a ghost it stands,
All in the dusk before day
That folds the dim lands:
Dark fell the skies when once belated,
Sad, and sorrow-fated, I missed the sun;
But wake, heart, and sing, for not in vain I waited.
O clear, O solemn dawning, lo, the maid is won!
Sweet dews, dry early on the grass and clover,
Lest the bride wet her feet while she walks over;
Shine to-day, sunbeams, and make all fair to see:
Down the dell she's coming — coming, coming with me.

A GLEANING SONG.

"WHITHER away, thou little careless rover?
(Kind Roger's true)
Whither away, across yon bents and clover,
Wet, wet with dew?"
"Roger here, Roger there —
Roger — O, he sighed,
Yet let me glean among the wheat,
Nor sit kind Roger's bride."

"What wilt thou do when all the gleaning's ended,
What wilt thou do?
The cold will come, and fog and frost-work blended
(Kind Roger's true)."

"Sleet and rain, cloud and storm,
 When they cease to frown
I'll bind me primrose bunches sweet,
 And cry them up the town."

"What if at last thy careless heart awaking
 This day thou rue?"
"I'll cry my flowers, and think for all its breaking,
 Kind Roger's true;
Roger here, Roger there,
 O, my true love sighed,
Sigh once, once more, I'll stay my feet
 And rest kind Roger's bride."

WITH A DIAMOND.

WHILE Time a grim old lion gnawing lay,
And mumbled with his teeth yon regal tomb,
Like some immortal tear undimmed for aye,
This gem was dropped among the dust of doom.

Dropped, haply, by a sad, forgotten queen,
A tear to outlast name, and fame, and tongue:
Her other tears, and ours, all tears terrene,
For great new griefs to be hereafter sung.

Take it, — a goddess might have wept such tears,
Or Dame Electra changed into a star,
That waxed so dim because her children's years
In leaguered Troy were bitter through long war.

Not till the end to end grow dull or waste, —
Ah, what a little while the light we share!
Hand after hand shall yet with this be graced,
Signing the Will that leaves it to an heir.

FANCY.

O FANCY, if thou flyest, come back anon,
Thy fluttering wings are soft as love's first word,
And fragrant as the feathers of that bird,
Which feeds upon the budded cinnamon.
I ask thee not to work, or sigh — play on,
From nought that was not, was, or is, deterred;
The flax that Old Fate spun thy flights have stirred,
And waved memorial grass of Marathon.
Play, but be gentle, not as on that day
I saw thee running down the rims of doom
With stars thou hadst been stealing — while they lay
Smothered in light and blue — clasped to thy breast;
Bring rather to me in the firelit room
A netted halcyon bird to sing of rest.

COMPENSATION.

ONE launched a ship, but she was wrecked at sea ;
He built a bridge, but floods have borne it down ;
He meant much good, none came : strange destiny,
His corn lies sunk, his bridge bears none to town,
Yet good he had not meant became his crown ;
For once at work, when even as nature free,
From thought of good he was, or of renown,
God took the work for good and let good be.
So wakened with a trembling after sleep,
Dread Mona Roa yields her fateful store ;
All gleaming hot the scarlet rivers creep,
And fanned of great-leaved palms slip to the shore,
Then stolen to unplumbed wastes of that far deep,
Lay the foundations for one island more.

LOOKING DOWN.

MOUNTAINS of sorrow, I have heard your moans,
And the moving of your pines; but we sit high
On your green shoulders, nearer stoops the sky,
And pure airs visit us from all the zones.
Sweet world beneath, too happy far to sigh,
Dost thou look thus beheld from heavenly thrones?
No; not for all the love that counts thy stones,
While sleepy with great light the valleys lie.
Strange, rapturous peace! its sunshine doth enfold
My heart; I have escaped to the days divine,
It seemeth as bygone ages back had rolled,
And all the eldest past was now, was mine;
Nay, even as if Melchizedec of old
Might here come forth to us with bread and wine.

Come, and in the woodland sit,
Seem a wonted part of it.

MARRIED LOVERS.

COME away, the clouds are high,
Put the flashing needles by.
Many days are not to spare,
Or to waste, my fairest fair!
All is ready. Come to-day,
For the nightingale her lay,
When she findeth that the whole
Of her love, and all her soul,
Cannot forth of her sweet throat,
Sobs the while she draws her breath,
And the bravery of her note
In a few days altereth.

Come, ere she despond, and see
In a silent ecstasy
Chestnuts heave for hours and hours
All the glory of their flowers

To the melting blue above,
That broods over them like love.
Leave the garden walls, where blow
Apple-blossoms pink, and low
Ordered beds of tulips fine.
Seek the blossoms made divine
With a scent that is their soul.
These are soulless. Bring the white
Of thy gown to bathe in light
Walls for narrow hearts. The whole
Earth is found, and air and sea,
Not too wide for thee and me.

Not too wide, and yet thy face
Gives the meaning of all space;
And thine eyes, with starbeams fraught,
Hold the measure of all thought;
For of them my soul besought,
And was shown a glimpse of thine —
A veiled vestal, with divine

Solace, in sweet love's despair,
For that life is brief as fair.
Who hath most, he yearneth most,
Sure, as seldom heretofore,
Somewhere of the gracious more.
Deepest joy the least shall boast,
Asking with new-opened eyes
The remainder; that which lies
O, so fair! but not all conned —
O, so near! and yet beyond.

Come, and in the woodland sit,
Seem a wonted part of it.
Then, while moves the delicate air,
And the glories of thy hair
Little flickering sun-rays strike,
Let me see what thou art like;
For great love enthralls me so,
That, in sooth, I scarcely know.

Show me, in a house all green,
Save for long gold wedges' sheen,
Where the flies, white sparks of fire,
Dart and hover and aspire,
And the leaves, air-stirred on high,
Feel such joy they needs must sigh,
And the untracked grass makes sweet
All fair flowers to touch thy feet,
And the bees about them hum.
All the world is waiting. Come!

A WINTER SONG.

CAME the dread Archer up yonder lawn—
Night is the time for the old to die—
But woe for an arrow that smote the fawn,
When the hind that was sick unscathed went by.

Father lay moaning, "Her fault was sore
(Night is the time when the old must die),
Yet, ah to bless her, my child, once more,
For heart is failing: the end is nigh."

"Daughter, my daughter, my girl," I cried
(Night is the time for the old to die)
"Woe for the wish if till morn ye bide"—
Dark was the welkin and wild the sky.

Heavily plunged from the roof the snow —
(Night is the time when the old will die),
She answered, "My mother, 'tis well, I go."
Sparkled the north star, the wrack flew high.

First at his head, and last at his feet
(Night is the time when the old should die),
Kneeling I watched till his soul did fleet,
None else that loved him, none else were nigh.

I wept in the night as the desolate weep
(Night is the time for the old to die),
Cometh my daughter? the drifts are deep,
Across the cold hollows how white they lie.

I sought her afar through the spectral trees
(Night is the time when the old must die),
The fells were all muffled, the floods did freeze,
And a wrathful moon hung red in the sky.

By night I found her where pent waves steal
  (Night is the time when the old should die),
But she lay stiff by the locked mill-wheel,
  And the old stars lived in their homes on high.

BINDING SHEAVES.

HARK! a lover binding sheaves
To his maiden sings,
Flutter, flutter go the leaves,
Larks drop their wings.
Little brooks for all their mirth
Are not blythe as he.
"Give me what the love is worth
That I give thee.

"Speech that cannot be forborne
Tells the story through:
I sowed my love in with the corn,
And they both grew.
Count the world full wide of girth,
And hived honey sweet,
But count the love of more worth
Laid at thy feet.

Hark ! a lover binding sheaves
  To his maiden sings ;
Flutter, flutter go the leaves,
  Larks drop their wings.

"Money's worth is house and land,
  Velvet coat and vest.
Work's worth is bread in hand,
  Ay, and sweet rest.
Wilt thou learn what love is worth?
  Ah! she sits above,
Sighing, 'Weigh me not with earth,
  Love's worth is love.'"

WORK.

LIKE coral insects multitudinous
The minutes are whereof our life is made.
They build it up as in the deep's blue shade
It grows, it comes to light, and then, and thus
For both there is an end. The populous
Sea-blossoms close, our minutes that have paid
Life's debt of work are spent; the work is laid
Before our feet that shall come after us.
We may not stay to watch if it will speed,
The bard if on some luter's string his song
Live sweetly yet; the hero if his star
Doth shine. Work is its own best earthly meed,
Else have we none more than the sea-born throng
Who wrought those marvellous isles that bloom afar.

WISHING.

WHEN I reflect how little I have done,
  And add to that how little I have seen,
Then furthermore how little I have won
  Of joy, or good, how little known, or been:
  I long for other life more full, more keen,
And yearn to change with such as well have run —
  Yet reason mocks me — nay, the soul, I ween,
Granted her choice would dare to change with none;
No, — not to feel, as Blondel when his lay
  Pierced the strong tower, and Richard answered it —
No, not to do, as Eustace on the day
  He left fair Calais to her weeping fit —
No, not to be, — Columbus, waked from sleep
When his new world rose from the charmèd deep.

TO ——.

STRANGE was the doom of Heracles, whose shade
  Had dwelling in dim Hades the unblest,
  While yet his form and presence sat a guest
With the old immortals when the feast was made.
Thine like, thus differs; form and presence laid
  In this dim chamber of enforcèd rest,
  It is the unseen "shade" which, risen, hath pressed
Above all heights where feet Olympian strayed.
My soul admires to hear thee speak; thy thought
  Falls from a high place like an August star,
Or some great eagle from his air-hung rings—
  When swooping past a snow-cold mountain scar—
Down the steep slope of a long sunbeam brought,
  He stirs the wheat with the steerage of his wings.

A cottager leaned whispering by her hives,
Telling the bees some news, as they lit down,
And entered one by one their waxen town.

ON THE BORDERS OF CANNOCK CHASE.

A COTTAGER leaned whispering by her hives,
  Telling the bees some news, as they lit down,
  And entered one by one their waxen town.
Larks passioning hung o'er their brooding wives,
And all the sunny hills where heather thrives
  Lay satisfied with peace. A stately crown
  Of trees enringed the upper headland brown,
And reedy pools, wherein the moor-hen dives,
Glittered and gleamed.
                                    A resting-place for light,
They that were bred here love it; but they say,
  "We shall not have it long; in three years' time
A hundred pits will cast out fires by night,
Down yon still glen their smoke shall trail its way,
  And the white ash lie thick in lieu of rime."

THE MARINER'S CAVE.

ONCE on a time there walked a mariner,
That had been shipwrecked; — on a lonely shore,
And the green water made a restless stir,
And a great flock of mews sped on before.
He had nor food nor shelter, for the tide
Rose on the one, and cliffs on the other side.

Brown cliffs they were; they seemed to pierce the sky,
That was an awful deep of empty blue,
Save that the wind was in it, and on high
A wavering skein of wild-fowl tracked it through.
He marked them not, but went with movement slow,
Because his thoughts were sad, his courage low.

His heart was numb, he neither wept nor sighed,
  But wearifully lingered by the wave;
Until at length it chanced that he espied,
  Far up, an opening in the cliff, a cave,
A shelter where to sleep in his distress,
And lose his sorrow in forgetfulness.

With that he clambered up the rugged face
  Of that steep cliff that all in shadow lay,
And, lo, there was a dry and homelike place,
  Comforting refuge for the castaway;
And he laid down his weary, weary head,
And took his fill of sleep till dawn waxed red.

When he awoke, warm stirring from the south
  Of delicate summer air did sough and flow;
He rose, and, wending to the cavern's mouth,
  He cast his eyes a little way below
Where on the narrow ledges, sharp and rude,
Preening their wings the blue rock-pigeons cooed.

Then he looked lower and saw the lavender
  And sea-thrift blooming in long crevices,
And the brown wallflower — April's messenger,
  The wallflower marshalled in her companies.
Then lower yet he looked adown the steep,
And sheer beneath him lapped the lovely deep.

The laughing deep ; — and it was pacified
  As if it had not raged that other day.
And it went murmuring in the morningtide
  Innumerable flatteries on its way,
Kissing the cliffs and whispering at their feet
With exquisite advancement, and retreat.

This when the mariner beheld he sighed,
  And thought on his companions lying low.
But while he gazed with eyes unsatisfied
  On the fair reaches of their overthrow,
Thinking it strange he only lived of all,
But not returning thanks, he heard a call !

A soft sweet call, a voice of tender ruth,
  He thought it came from out the cave. And, lo,
It whispered, "Man, look up!" But he, forsooth,
  Answered, "I cannot, for the long waves flow
Across my gallant ship where sunk she lies
With all my riches and my merchandise.

"Moreover, I am heavy for the fate
  Of these my mariners drowned in the deep;
I must lament me for their sad estate
  Now they are gathered in their last long sleep.
O! the unpitying heavens upon me frown,
Then how should I look up?—I must look down."

And he stood yet watching the fair green sea
  Till hunger reached him; then he made a fire,
A driftwood fire, and wandered listlessly
  And gathered many eggs at his desire,
And dressed them for his meal, and then he lay
And slept, and woke upon the second day.

Whenas he said, "The cave shall be my home;
None will molest me, for the brown cliffs rise
Like castles of defence behind, — the foam
Of the remorseless sea beneath me lies;
'Tis easy from the cliff my food to win —
The nations of the rock-dove breed therein.

"For fuel, at the ebb yon fair expanse
Is strewed with driftwood by the breaking wave,
And in the sea is fish for sustenance.
I will build up the entrance of the cave,
And leave therein a window and a door,
And here will dwell and leave it nevermore."

Then even so he did; and when his task,
Many long days being over, was complete;
When he had eaten, as he sat to bask
In the red firelight glowing at his feet,
He was right glad of shelter, and he said,
"Now for my comrades am I comforted."

Then did the voice awake and speak again ;
  It murmured, "Man, look up!" But he replied,
"I cannot. O, mine eyes, mine eyes are fain
  Down on the red wood-ashes to abide
Because they warm me." Then the voice was still,
And left the lonely mariner to his will.

And soon it came to pass that he got gain.
  He had great flocks of pigeons which he fed,
And drew great store of fish from out the main,
  And down from eiderducks ; and then he said,
"It is not good that I should lead my life
In silence, I will take to me a wife."

He took a wife, and brought her home to him ;
  And he was good to her and cherished her
So that she loved him ; then when light waxed dim
  Gloom came no more ; and she would minister
To all his wants ; while he, being well content,
Counted her company right excellent.

But once as on the lintel of the door
  She leaned to watch him while he put to sea,
This happy wife, down-gazing at the shore,
  Said sweetly, "It is better now with me
Than it was lately when I used to spin
In my old father's house beside the lin."

And then the soft voice of the cave awoke —
  The soft voice which had haunted it erewhile —
And gently to the wife it also spoke,
  "Woman, look up!" But she, with tender guile,
Gave it denial, answering, "Nay, not so,
For all that I should look on lieth below.

"The great sky overhead is not so good
  For my two eyes as yonder stainless sea,
The source and yielder of our livelihood,
  Where rocks his little boat that loveth me."
This when the wife had said she moved away,
And looked no higher than the wave all day.

Now when the year ran out a child she bore,
  And there was such rejoicing in the cave
As surely never had there been before
  Since God first made it. Then full, sweet, and grave,
The voice, "God's utmost blessing brims thy cup,
O, father of this child, look up, look up!"

"Speak to my wife," the mariner replied.
  "I have much work — right welcome work 'tis true —
Another mouth to feed." And then it sighed,
  "Woman, look up!" She said, "Make no ado,
For I must needs look down, on anywise,
My heaven is in the blue of these dear eyes."

The seasons of the year did swiftly whirl,
  They measured time by one small life alone;
On such a day the pretty pushing pearl
  That mouth they loved to kiss had sweetly shown,
That smiling mouth, and it had made essay
To give them names on such another day.

And afterward his infant history,
  Whether he played with baubles on the floor,
Or crept to pat the rock-doves pecking nigh,
  And feeding on the threshold of the door,
They loved to mark, and all his marvellings dim,
The mysteries that beguiled and baffled him.

He was so sweet, that oft his mother said,
  "O, child, how was it that I dwelt content
Before thou camest? Blessings on thy head,
  Thy pretty talk it is so innocent,
That oft for all my joy, though it be deep,
When thou art prattling, I am like to weep."

Summer and winter spent themselves again,
  The rock-doves in their season bred, the cliff
Grew sweet, for every cleft would entertain
  Its tuft of blossom, and the mariner's skiff,
Early and late, would linger in the bay,
Because the sea was calm and winds away.

The little child about that rocky height,
  Led by her loving hand who gave him birth,
Might wander in the clear unclouded light,
  And take his pastime in the beauteous earth;
Smell the fair flowers in stony cradles swung,
And see God's happy creatures feed their young.

And once it came to pass, at eventide,
  His mother set him in the cavern door,
And filled his lap with grain, and stood aside
  To watch the circling rock-doves soar, and soar,
Then dip, alight, and run in circling bands,
To take the barley from his open hands.

And even while she stood and gazed at him,
  And his grave father's eyes upon him dwelt,
They heard the tender voice, and it was dim,
  And seemed full softly in the air to melt;
"Father," it murmured, "Mother," dying away,
"Look up, while yet the hours are called to-day."

"I will," the father answered, "but not now;"
  The mother said, "Sweet voice, O speak to me
At a convenient season." And the brow
  Of the cliff began to quake right fearfully,
There was a rending crash, and there did leap
A riven rock and plunge into the deep.

They said, "A storm is coming;" but they slept
  That night in peace, and thought the storm had passed,
For there was not a cloud to intercept
  The sacred moonlight on the cradle cast;
And to his rocking boat at dawn of day,
With joy of heart the mariner took his way.

But when he mounted up the path at night,
  Foreboding not of trouble or mischance,
His wife came out into the fading light,
  And met him with a serious countenance;
And she broke out in tears and sobbings thick,
"The child is sick, my little child is sick."

They knelt beside him in the sultry dark,
  And when the moon looked in his face was pale,
And when the red sun, like a burning barque,
  Rose in a fog at sea, his tender wail
Sank deep into their hearts, and piteously
They fell to chiding of their destiny.

The doves unheeded cooed that livelong day,
  Their pretty playmate cared for them no more;
The sea-thrift nodded, wet with glistening spray,
  None gathered it; the long wave washed the shore;
He did not know, nor lift his eyes to trace,
The new fallen shadow in his dwelling-place.

The sultry sun beat on the cliffs all day,
  And hot calm airs slept on the polished sea,
The mournful mother wore her time away,
  Bemoaning of her helpless misery,
Pleading and plaining, till the day was done,
O look on me, my love, my little one.

"What aileth thee, that thou dost lie and moan?
Ah would that I might bear it in thy stead."
The father made not his forebodings known,
But gazed, and in his secret soul he said,
"I may have sinned, on sin waits punishment,
But as for him, sweet blameless innocent,

"What has he done that he is stricken down?
O it is hard to see him sink and fade,
When I, that counted him my dear life's crown,
So willingly have worked while he has played;
That he might sleep, have risen, come storm, come heat,
And thankfully would fast that he might eat."

My God, how short our happy days appear!
How long the sorrowful! They thought it long,
The sultry morn that brought such evil cheer,
And sat, and wished, and sighed for evensong;
It came, and cooling wafts about him stirred,
Yet when they spoke he answered not a word.

"Take heart," they cried, but their sad hearts sank low
  When he would moan and turn his restless head,
And wearily the lagging morns would go,
  And nights, while they sat watching by his bed,
Until a storm came up with wind and rain,
And lightning ran along the troubled main.

Over their heads the mighty thunders brake,
  Leaping and tumbling down from rock to rock;
Then burst anew and made the cliffs to quake
  As they were living things and felt the shock;
The waiting sea to sob as if in pain,
And all the midnight vault to ring again.

  lamp was burning in the mariner's cave,
  But the blue lightning flashes made it dim;
And when the mother heard those thunders rave,
  She took her little child to cherish him;
She took him in her arms, and on her breast
Full wearily she courted him to rest,

And soothed him long until the storm was spent,
  And the last thunder peal had died away,
And stars were out in all the firmament.
  Then did he cease to moan, and slumbering lay,
While in the welcome silence, pure and deep,
The care-worn parents sweetly fell asleep.

And in a dream, enwrought with fancies thick,
  The mother thought she heard the rock-doves coo
(She had forgotten that her child was sick),
  And she went forth their morning meal to strew;
Then over all the cliff with earnest care
She sought her child, and lo, he was not there!

But she was not afraid, though long she sought
  And climbed the cliff, and set her feet in grass,
Then reached a river, broad and full, she thought,
  And at its brink he sat. Alas! alas!
For one stood near him, fair and undefiled,
An innocent, a marvellous man-child.

In garments white as wool, and O, most fair,
  A rainbow covered him with mystic light;
Upon the warmèd grass his feet were bare,
  And as he breathed, the rainbow in her sight
In passions of clear crimson trembling lay,
With gold and violet mist made fair the day.

Her little life! she thought, his little hands
  Were full of flowers that he did play withal;
But when he saw the boy o' the golden lands,
  And looked him in the face, he let them fall,
Held through a rapturous pause in wistful wise
To the sweet strangeness of those keen child-eyes.

"Ah, dear and awful God, who chastenest me,
  How shall my soul to this be reconciled.
It is the Saviour of the world," quoth she,
  "And to my child He cometh as a child."
Then on her knees she fell by that vast stream —
Oh, it was sorrowful, this woman's dream!

For lo, that Elder Child drew nearer now,
  Fair as the light, and purer than the sun.
The calms of heaven were brooding on his brow,
  And in his arms He took her little one,
Her child, that knew her, but with sweet demur
Drew back, nor held his hands to come to her.

With that in mother misery sore she wept—
  "O Lamb of God, I love my child so MUCH!
He stole away to Thee while we two slept,
  But give him back, for Thou hast many such;
And as for me I have but one. O deign,
Dear Pity of God, to give him me again."

His feet were on the river. Oh, his feet
  Had touched the river now, and it was great;
And yet He hearkened when she did entreat,
  And turned in quietness as He would wait—
Wait till she looked upon Him, and behold,
There lay a long way off a city of gold.

Like to a jasper and a sardine stone,
  Whelmed in the rainbow stood that fair man-child,
Mighty and innocent, that held her own,
  And as might be his manner at home he smiled,
Then while she looked and looked, the vision brake,
And all amazed she started up awake.

And lo, her little child was gone indeed!
  The sleep that knows no waking he had slept,
Folded to heaven's own heart; in rainbow brede
  Clothed and made glad, while they two mourned and wept,
But in the drinking of their bitter cup
The sweet voice spoke once more, and sighed, "Look up!"

They heard, and straightway answered, "Even so:
  For what abides that we should look on here?
The heavens are better than this earth below,
  They are of more account and far more dear.
We will look up, for all most sweet and fair,
Most pure, most excellent, is garnered there."

A REVERIE.

WHEN I do sit apart
And commune with my heart,
She brings me forth the treasures once my own;
Shows me a happy place
Where leaf-buds swelled apace,
And wasting rims of snow in sunlight shone.

Rock, in a mossy glade,
The larch-trees lend thee shade,
That just begin to feather with their leaves;
From out thy crevice deep
White tufts of snowdrops peep,
And melted rime drips softly from thine eaves.

Once to that cottage door,
In happy days of yore,
My little love made footprints in the snow.
She was so glad of spring,
She helped birds to sing.

Ah, rock, I know, I know
That yet thy snowdrops grow,
And yet doth sunshine fleck them through the tree,
Whose sheltering branches hide
The cottage at its side,
That nevermore will shade or shelter me.

I know the stockdoves' note
Athwart the glen doth float:
With sweet foreknowledge of her twins oppressed,
And longings onward sent,
She broods before the event,
While leisurely she mends her shallow nest.

Once to that cottage door,
In happy days of yore,
My little love made footprints in the snow.
She was so glad of spring,
She helped the birds to sing,
I know she dwells there yet — the rest I do not know.

They sang, and would not stop,
While drop, and drop, and drop,
I heard the melted rime in sunshine fall;
And narrow wandering rills,
Where leaned the daffodils,
Murmured and murmured on, and that was all.

I think, but cannot tell,
I think she loved me well,
And some dear fancy with my future twined.
But I shall never know,
Hope faints, and lets it go,
That passionate want forbid to speak its mind.

DEFTON WOOD.

I HELD my way through Defton Wood,
  And on to Wandor Hall;
The dancing leaf let down the light,
  In hovering spots to fall.
"O young, young leaves, you match me well,"
  My heart was merry, and sung—
"Now wish me joy of my sweet youth;
  My love—she, too, is young!
    O so many, many, many
      Little homes above my head!
    O so many, many, many
      Dancing blossoms round me spread!
    O so many, many, many
      Maidens sighing yet for none!
    Speed, ye wooers, speed with any—
      Speed with all but one."

I took my leave of Wandor Hall,
  And trod the woodland ways.
"What shall I do so long to bear
  The burden of my days?"
I sighed my heart into the boughs
  Whereby the culvers cooed;
For only I between them went
  Unwooing and unwooed.
    "O so many, many, many
      Lilies bending stately heads!
    O so many, many, many
      Strawberries ripened on their beds!
    O so many, many, many
      Maids, and yet my heart undone!
    What to me are all, are any —
      I have lost my — one."

THE SNOWDROP MONUMENT (IN LICHFIELD CATHEDRAL).

Marvels of sleep, grown cold!
Who hath not longed to fold
With pitying ruth, forgetful of their bliss,
Those cherub forms that lie,
With none to watch them nigh,
Or touch the silent lips with one warm human kiss?

What! they are left alone
All night with graven stone,
Pillars and arches that above them meet;
While through those windows high
The journeying stars can spy,
And dim blue moonbeams drop on their uncovered feet?

O cold! yet look again,
There is a wandering vein
Traced in the hand where those white snowdrops lie.
Let her rapt dreamy smile
The wondering heart beguile,
That almost thinks to hear a calm contented sigh.

What silence dwells between
Those severed lips serene!
The rapture of sweet waiting breathes and grows.
What trance-like peace is shed
On her reclining head,
And e'en on listless feet what languor of repose!

Angels of joy and love
Lean softly from above
And whisper to her sweet and marvellous things;
Tell of the golden gate
That opened wide doth wait,
And shadow her dim sleep with their celestial wings.

Hearing of that blest shore
She thinks on earth no more,
Contented to forego this wintry land.
She has nor thought nor care
But to rest calmly there,
And hold the snowdrops pale that blossom in her hand.

But on the other face
Broodeth a mournful grace,
This had foreboding thoughts beyond her years,
While sinking thus to sleep
She saw her mother weep,
And could not lift her hand to dry those heart-sick tears.

Could not — but failing lay,
Sighed her young life away,
And let her arm drop down in listless rest,
Too weary on that bed
To turn her dying head,
Or fold the little sister nearer to her breast.

Yet this is faintly told
On features fair and cold,
A look of calm surprise, of meek regret,
As if with life oppressed
She turned her to her rest,
But felt her mother's love and looked not to forget.

How wistfully they close,
Sweet eyes, to their repose!
How quietly declines the placid brow!
The young lips seem to say,
"I have wept much to-day,
And felt some bitter pains, but they are over now."

Sleep! there are left below
Many who pine to go,
Many who lay it to their chastened souls,
That gloomy days draw nigh,
And they are blest who die,
For this green world grows worse the longer that she
rolls.

And as for me I know
A little of her woe,
Her yearning want doth in my soul abide,
And sighs of them that weep,
" O put us soon to sleep,
For when we wake — with Thee — we shall be satisfied."

AN ANCIENT CHESS KING.

HAPLY some Rajah first in the ages gone
Amid his languid ladies fingered thee,
While a black nightingale, sun-swart as he,
Sang his one wife, love's passionate oraison;
Haply thou may'st have pleased Old Prester John
Among his pastures, when full royally
He sat in tent, grave shepherds at his knee,
While lamps of balsam winked and glimmered on.
What doest thou here? Thy masters are all dead;
My heart is full of ruth and yearning pain
At sight of thee; O king that hast a crown
Outlasting theirs, and tell'st of greatness fled
Through cloud-hung nights of unabated rain
And murmurs of the dark majestic town.

COMFORT IN THE NIGHT.

SHE thought by heaven's high wall that she did stray
  Till she beheld the everlasting gate:
  And she climbed up to it to long, and wait,
Feel with her hands (for it was night), and lay
Her lips to it with kisses; thus to pray
  That it might open to her desolate.
  And lo! it trembled, lo! her passionate
Crying prevailed. A little little way
It opened: there fell out a thread of light,
  And she saw wingèd wonders move within;
Also she heard sweet talking as they meant
To comfort her. They said, "Who comes to-night
  Shall one day certainly an entrance win;"
Then the gate closed and she awoke content.

THOUGH ALL GREAT DEEDS.

THOUGH all great deeds were proved but fables fine,
Though earth's old story could be told anew,
Though the sweet fashions loved of them that sue
Were empty as the ruined Delphian shrine —
Though God did never man, in words benign,
With sense of His great Fatherhood endue,
Though life immortal were a dream untrue,
And He that promised it were not divine —
Though soul, though spirit were not, and all hope
Reaching beyond the bourne, melted away;
Though virtue had no goal and good no scope,
But both were doomed to end with this our clay —
Though all these were not, — to the ungraced heir
Would this remain, — to live, as though they were.

THE LONG WHITE SEAM.

AS I came round the harbor buoy,
The lights began to gleam,
No wave the land-locked water stirred,
The crags were white as cream;
And I marked my love by candle-light
Sewing her long white seam.
It's aye sewing ashore, my dear,
Watch and steer at sea,
It's reef and furl, and haul the line,
Set sail and think of thee.

I climbed to reach her cottage door;
O sweetly my love sings!
Like a shaft of light her voice breaks forth,
My soul to meet it springs
As the shining water leaped of old,
When stirred by angel wings.

Aye longing to list anew,
Awake and in my dream,
But never a song she sang like this,
Sewing her long white seam.

Fair fall the lights, the harbor lights,
That brought me in to thee,
And peace drop down on that low roof
For the sight that I did see,
And the voice, my dear, that rang so clear
All for the love of me.
For O, for O, with brows bent low
By the candle's flickering gleam,
Her wedding gown it was she wrought,
Sewing the long white seam.

AN OLD WIFE'S SONG.

AND what will ye hear, my daughters dear? —
Oh, what will ye hear this night?
Shall I sing you a song of the yuletide cheer,
Or of lovers and ladies bright?

"Thou shalt sing," they say (for we dwell far away
From the land where fain would we be),
"Thou shalt sing us again some old-world strain
That is sung in our own countrie.

"Thou shalt mind us so of the times long ago,
When we walked on the upland lea,
While the old harbor light waxed faint in the white,
Long rays shooting out from the sea;

"While lambs were yet asleep, and the dew lay deep
  On the grass, and their fleeces clean and fair.
Never grass was seen so thick nor so green
  As the grass that grew up there!

"In the town was no smoke, for none there awoke—
  At our feet it lay still as still could be;
And we saw far below the long river flow,
  And the schooners a-warping out to sea.

"Sing us now a strain shall make us feel again
  As we felt in that sacred peace of morn,
When we had the first view of the wet sparkling dew.,
  In the shyness of a day just born."

So I sang an old song—it was plain and not long—
  I had sung it very oft when they were small;
And long ere it was done they wept every one:
  Yet this was all the song—this was all:—

The snow lies white, and the moon gives light,
  I'll out to the freezing mere,
And ease my heart with one little song,
  For none will be nigh to hear.
  And it's O my love, my love!
  And it's O my dear, my dear!
It's of her that I'll sing till the wild woods ring,
  When nobody's nigh to hear.

My love is young, she is young, is young;
  When she laughs the dimple dips.
We walked in the wind, and her long locks blew
  Till sweetly they touched my lips.
  And I'll out to the freezing mere,
  Where the stiff reeds whistle so low,
And I'll tell my mind to the friendly wind,
  Because I have loved her so.

Ay, and she's true, my lady is true!
  And that's the best of it all;

And when she blushes my heart so yearns
  That tears are ready to fall.
  And it's O my love, my love!
  And it's O my dear, my dear!
It's of her that I'll sing till the wild woods ring,
  When nobody's nigh to hear.

COLD AND QUIET.

COLD, my dear, — cold and quiet.
In their cups on yonder lea,
Cowslips fold the brown bee's diet;
So the moss enfoldeth thee.
"Plant me, plant me, O love, a lily flower —
Plant at my head, I pray you, a green tree;
And when our children sleep," she sighed, "at the dusk hour,
And when the lily blossoms, O come out to me!"

Lost, my dear? Lost! nay, deepest
Love is that which loseth least;
Through the night-time while thou sleepest,
Still I watch the shrouded east.

Near thee, near thee, my wife that aye liveth,
  "Lost" is no word for such a love as mine;
Love from her past to me a present giveth,
  And love itself doth comfort, making pain divine.
    Rest, my dear, rest. Fair showeth
      That which was, and not in vain
    Sacred have I kept, God knoweth,
      Love's last words atween us twain.
"Hold by our past, my only love, my lover;
  Fall not, but rise, O love, by loss of me!"
Boughs from our garden, white with bloom hang over.
  Love, now the children slumber, I come out to thee.

A SNOW MOUNTAIN.

CAN I make white enough my thought for thee,
Or wash my words in light? Thou hast no mate
To sit aloft in the silence silently
And twin those matchless heights undesecrate.
Reverend as Lear, when, lorn of shelter, he
Stood, with his old white head, surprised at fate;
Alone as Galileo, when, set free,
Before the stars he mused disconsolate.
Ay, and remote, as the dead lords of song,
Great masters who have made us what we are,
For thou and they have taught us how to long
And feel a sacred want of the fair and far:
Reign, and keep life in this our deep desire —
Our only greatness is that we aspire.

SLEEP.

(A WOMAN SPEAKS.)

O SLEEP, we are beholden to thee, sleep,
Thou bearest angels to us in the night,
Saints out of heaven with palms. Seen by thy light
Sorrow is some old tale that goeth not deep;
Love is a pouting child. Once I did sweep
Through space with thee, and lo, a dazzling sight—
Stars! They came on, I felt their drawing and might;
And some had dark companions. Once (I weep
When I remember that) we sailed the tide,
And found fair isles, where no isles used to bide,
And met there my lost love, who said to me,
That 'twas a long mistake: he had not died.
Sleep, in the world to come how strange 'twill be
Never to want, never to wish for thee!

PROMISING.

(A MAN SPEAKS.)

Once, a new world, the sunswart marinere,
Columbus, promised, and was sore withstood,
Ungraced, unhelped, unheard for many a year;
But let at last to make his promise good.
Promised and promising I go, most dear,
To better my dull heart with love's sweet feud,
My life with its most reverent hope and fear,
And my religion, with fair gratitude.
O we must part; the stars for me contend,
And all the winds that blow on all the seas.
Through wonderful waste places I must wend,
And with a promise my sad soul appease.
Promise then, promise much of far-off bliss;
But — ah, for present joy, give me one kiss.

LOVE.

Who veileth love should first have vanquished fate.
She folded up the dream in her deep heart,
Her fair full lips were silent on that smart,
Thick fringèd eyes did on the grasses wait.
What good? one eloquent blush, but one, and straight
The meaning of a life was known; for art
Is often foiled in playing nature's part,
And time holds nothing long inviolate.
Earth's buried seed springs up — slowly, or fast:
The ring came home, that one in ages past
Flung to the keeping of unfathomed seas:
And golden apples on the mystic trees
Were sought and found, and borne away at last,
Though watched of the divine Hesperides.

POEMS

Written on the Deaths of Three Lovely Children who were taken from their Parents within a Month of one another.

HENRY,

AGED EIGHT YEARS.

YELLOW leaves, how fast they flutter — woodland hollows thickly strewing,
Where the wan October sunbeams scantly in the mid-day win,
While the dim gray clouds are drifting, and in saddened hues imbuing
All without and all within!

All within! but winds of autumn, little Henry, round their dwelling
Did not load your father's spirit with those deep and burdened sighs; —
Only echoed thoughts of sadness, in your mother's bosom swelling,
Fast as tears that dim her eyes.

Life is fraught with many changes, checked with sorrow and mutation,
But no grief it ever lightened such a truth before to know: —
I behold them — father, mother — as they seemed to contemplation,
Only three short weeks ago!

Saddened for the morrow's parting — up the stairs at midnight stealing —
As with cautious foot we glided past the children's open door, —

"Come in here," they said, the lamplight dimpled forms
at last revealing,
"Kiss them in their sleep once more."

You were sleeping, little Henry, with your eyelids
scarcely closing,
Two sweet faces near together, with their rounded
arms entwined: —
And the rose-bud lips were moving, as if stirred in their
reposing
By the movements of the mind!

And your mother smoothed the pillow, and her sleeping
treasures numbered,
Whispering fondly — "He is dreaming" — as you
turned upon your bed —
And your father stooped to kiss you, happy dreamer, as
you slumbered,
With his hand upon your head!

Did he know the true deep meaning of his blessing?
No! he never
Heard afar the summons uttered—"Come up hither"
—Never knew
How the awful Angel faces kept his sleeping boy for ever,
And for ever in their view.

Awful Faces, unimpassioned, silent Presences were by us,
Shrouding wings—majestic beings—hidden by this earthly veil—
Such as we have called on, saying, "Praise the Lord, O Ananias,
Azarias and Misael!"

But we saw not, and who knoweth, what the missioned Spirits taught him,
To that one small bed drawn nearer, when we left him to their will?

While he slumbered, who can answer for what dreams
they may have brought him,
When at midnight all was still?

Father! Mother! must you leave him on his bed, but not
to slumber?
Are the small hands meekly folded on his breast, but
not to pray?
When you count your children over, must you tell a
different number,
Since that happier yesterday?

Father! Mother! weep if need be, since this is a "time"
for weeping,
Comfort comes not for the calling, grief is never argued
down—
Coldly sounds the admonition, "Why lament? in better
keeping
Rests the child than in your own."

"Truth indeed! but, oh! compassion! Have you sought
to scan my sorrow?"
(Mother, you shall meekly ponder, list'ning to that
common tale)
"Does your heart repeat its echo, or by fellow-feeling
borrow
Even a tone that might avail?

"Might avail to steal it from me, by its deep heart-warm
affection?
Might perceive by strength of loving how the fond
words to combine?
Surely no! I will be silent, in your soul is no reflection
Of the care that burdens mine!"

When the winter twilight gathers, Father, and your
thoughts shall wander,
Sitting lonely you shall blend him with your listless
reveries,
Half forgetful what division holds the form whereon you
ponder
From its place upon your knees—

With a start of recollection, with a half-reproachful
wonder,
Of itself the heart shall question, "Art Thou then no
longer here?
Is it so, my little Henry? Are we set so far asunder
Who were wont to be so near?"

While the fire-light dimly flickers, and the lengthened
shades are meeting,
To itself the heart shall answer, "He shall come to
me no more:
I shall never hear his footsteps nor the child's sweet
voice entreating
For admission at my door."

But upon *your* fair, fair forehead, no regrets nor griefs
are dwelling,
Neither sorrow nor disquiet do the peaceful features
know;
Nor that look, whose wistful beauty seemed their sad
hearts to be telling,
"Daylight breaketh, let me go!"

Daylight breaketh, little Henry; in its beams your soul awaketh —
What though night should close around us, dim and dreary to the view —
Though *our* souls should walk in darkness, far away that morning breaketh
Into endless day for you!

SAMUEL,

AGED NINE YEARS.

THEY have left you, little Henry, but they have not left you lonely —
Brothers' hearts so knit together could not, might not separate dwell,
Fain to seek you in the mansions far away — One lingered only
To bid those behind farewell!

Gentle Boy! — His childlike nature in most guileless
form was moulded,
And it may be that his spirit woke in glory unaware,
Since so calmly he resigned it, with his hands still
meekly folded,
Having said his evening prayer.

Or — if conscious of that summons — "Speak, O Lord,
Thy servant heareth" —
As one said, whose name they gave him, might his
willing answer be,
"Here am I" — like him replying — "At Thy gates my
soul appeareth,
For behold Thou calledst me!"

A deep silence — utter silence, on his earthly home de-
scendeth: —
Reading, playing, sleeping, waking — he is gone, and
few remain!
"O the loss!" — they utter, weeping — every voice its
echo lendeth —
"O the loss!" — But, O the gain!

On that tranquil shore his spirit was vouchsafed an early landing,
Lest the toils of crime should stain it, or the thrall of guilt control —
Lest that "wickedness should alter the yet simple understanding,
Or deceit beguile his soul!"

"Lay not up on earth thy treasure" — they have read that sentence duly,
Moth and rust shall fret thy riches — earthly good hath swift decay —
"Even so," each heart replieth — "As for me, my riches truly
Make them wings and flee away!"

"O my riches! — O my children! — dearest part of life and being,
Treasures looked to for the solace of this life's declining years, —

Were our voices cold to hearing — or our faces cold to seeing,
That ye left us to our tears?"

"We inherit conscious silence, ceasing of some merry laughter,
And the hush of two sweet voices — (healing sounds for spirits bruised!)
Of the tread of joyous footsteps in the pathway following after,
Of two names no longer used!"

Question for them, little Sister, in your sweet and childish fashion —
Search and seek them, Baby Brother, with your calm and asking eyes —
Dimpled lips that fail to utter fond appeal or sad compassion,
Mild regret or dim surprise!

There are two tall trees above you, by the high east window growing,
Underneath them, slumber sweetly, lapt in silence deep, serene;
Save, when pealing in the distance, organ notes towards you flowing
Echo — with a pause between!

And that pause? — a voice shall fill it — tones that blessed you daily, nightly,
Well beloved, but not sufficing, Sleepers, to awake you now,
Though so near he stand, that shadows from your trees may tremble lightly
On his book and on his brow!

Sleep then ever! Neither singing of sweet birds shall break your slumber,
Neither fall of dew, nor sunshine, dance of leaves, nor drift of snow,

Charm those dropt lids more to open, nor the tranquil bosoms cumber
With one care for things below!

It is something, the assurance, that *you* ne'er shall feel like sorrow,
Weep no past and dread no future — know not sighing, feel not pain —
Nor a day that looketh forward to a mournfuller to-morrow —
"Clouds returning after rain!"

No, far off, the daylight breaketh, in its beams each soul awaketh:
"What though clouds," they sigh, "be gathered dark and stormy to the view,
Though the light our eyes forsaketh, fresh and sweet behold it breaketh
Into endless day for you!"

KATIE, AGED FIVE YEARS.

(ASLEEP IN THE DAYTIME.)

ALL rough winds are hushed and silent, golden light the meadow steepeth,
And the last October roses daily wax more pale and fair;
They have laid a gathered blossom on the breast of one who sleepeth
With a sunbeam on her hair.

Calm, and draped in snowy raiment she lies still, as one that dreameth,
And a grave sweet smile hath parted dimpled lips that may not speak;
Slanting down that narrow sunbeam like a ray of glory gleameth
On the sainted brow and cheek.

There is silence! They who watch her, speak no word
of grief or wailing,
In a strange unwonted calmness they gaze on and cannot cease,
Though the pulse of life beat faintly, thought shrink
back, and hope be failing,
They, like Aaron, "hold their peace."

While they gaze on her, the deep bell with its long slow
pauses soundeth;
Long they hearken — father — mother — love has nothing more to say:
Beating time to feet of Angels leading her where love
aboundeth
Tolls the heavy bell this day.

Still in silence to its tolling they count over all her
meetness
To lie near their hearts and soothe them in all sorrows
and all fears;

Her short life lies spread before them, but they cannot tell her sweetness,
Easily as tell her years.

Only daughter — Ah! how fondly Thought around that lost name lingers,
Oft when lone your mother sitteth, she shall weep and droop her head,
She shall mourn her baby-sempstress, with those imitative fingers,
Drawing out her aimless thread.

In your father's Future cometh many a sad uncheered to-morrow,
But in sleep shall three fair faces heavenly-calm towards him lean —
Like a threefold cord shall draw him through the weariness of sorrow,
Nearer to the things unseen.

With the closing of your eyelids close the dreams of expectation,
And so ends the fairest chapter in the records of their way:
Therefore — O thou God most holy — God of rest and consolation,
Be Thou near to them this day!

Be Thou near, when they shall nightly, by the bed of infant brothers,
Hear their soft and gentle breathing, and shall bless them on their knees;
And shall think how coldly falleth the white moonlight on the others,
In their bed beneath the trees.

Be Thou near, when they, they *only*, bear those faces in remembrance,
And the number of their children strangers ask them with a smile;

And when other childlike faces touch them by the strong resemblance
To those turned to them erewhile.

Be Thou near, each chastened Spirit for its course and conflict nerving,
Let Thy voice say, "Father — mother — lo! thy treasures live above!
Now be strong, be strong, no longer cumbered overmuch with serving
At the shrine of human love."

Let them sleep! In course of ages e'en the Holy House shall crumble,
And the broad and stately steeple one day bend to its decline,
And high arches, ancient arches bowed and decked in clothing humble,
Creeping moss shall round them twine.

Ancient arches, old and hoary, sunny beams shall glimmer through them,
And invest them with a beauty we would fain they should not share,
And the moonlight slanting down them, the white moonlight shall imbue them
With a sadness dim and fair.

Then the soft green moss shall wrap you, and the world shall all forget you,
Life, and stir, and toil, and tumult unawares shall pass you by;
Generations come and vanish: but it shall not grieve nor fret you,
That they sin, or that they sigh.

And the world, grown old in sinning, shall deny her first beginning,
And think scorn of words which whisper how that all must pass away;

Time's arrest and intermission shall account a vain tradition,
And a dream, the reckoning day!

Till His blast, a blast of terror, shall awake in shame and sadness
Faithless millions to a vision of the failing earth and skies,
And more sweet than song of Angels, in their shout of joy and gladness,
Call the dead in Christ to rise!

Then, by One Man's intercession, standing clear from their transgression,
Father — mother — you shall meet them fairer than they were before,
And have joy with the Redeemèd, joy ear hath not heard — heart dreamèd,
Ay for ever — evermore!

Fair Margaret, who sittest all day long
On the grey stone beneath the sycamore.

THE TWO MARGARETS.

I.

MARGARET BY THE MERE SIDE.

LYING imbedded in the green champaigne
That gives no shadow to thy silvery face,
Open to all the heavens, and all their train,
The marshalled clouds that cross with stately pace,
No steadfast hills on thee reflected rest,
Nor waver with the dimpling of thy breast.

O, silent Mere! about whose marges spring
Thick bulrushes to hide the reed-bird's nest;
Where the shy ousel dips her glossy wing,
And balanced in the water takes her rest:
While under bending leaves, all gem-arrayed,
Blue dragon-flies sit panting in the shade:

Warm, stilly place, the sundew loves thee well,
  And the green sward comes creeping to thy brink,
And golden saxifrage and pimpernel
  Lean down to thee their perfumed heads to drink;
And heavy with the weight of bees doth bend
White clover, and beneath thy wave descend:

While the sweet scent of bean-fields, floated wide
  On a long eddy of the lightsome air
Over the level mead to thy lone side,
  Doth lose itself among thy zephyrs rare,
With wafts from hawthorn bowers and new-cut hay,
And blooming orchards lying far away.

Thou hast thy Sabbaths, when a deeper calm
  Descends upon thee, quiet Mere, and then
There is a sound of bells, a far-off psalm
  From gray church towers, that swims across the fen;
And the light sigh where grass and waters meet,
Is thy meek welcome to the visit sweet.

Thou hast thy lovers. Though the angler's rod
  Dimple thy surface seldom ; though the oar
Fill not with silvery globes thy fringing sod,
  Nor send long ripples to thy lonely shore ;
Though few, as in a glass, have cared to trace
The smile of nature moving on thy face ;

Thou hast thy lovers truly. 'Mid the cold
  Of northern tarns the wild-fowl dream of thee,
And, keeping thee in mind, their wings unfold,
  And shape their course, high soaring, till they see
Down in the world, like molten silver, rest
Their goal, and screaming plunge them in thy breast.

Fair Margaret, who sittest all day long
  On the gray stone beneath the sycamore,
The bowering tree with branches lithe and strong,
  The only one to grace the level shore,
Why dost thou wait? for whom with patient cheer
Gaze yet so wistfully adown the Mere?

Thou canst not tell, thou dost not know, alas!
  Long watchings leave behind them little trace;
And yet how sweetly must the mornings pass,
  That bring that dreamy calmness to thy face!
How quickly must the evenings come that find
Thee still regret to leave the Mere behind!

Thy cheek is resting on thy hand; thine eyes
  Are like twin violets but half unclosed,
And quiet as the deeps in yonder skies.
  Never more peacefully in love reposed
A mother's gaze upon her offspring dear,
Than thine upon the long far-stretching Mere.

Sweet innocent! Thy yellow hair floats low
  In rippling undulations on thy breast,
Then stealing down the parted love-locks flow,
  Bathed in a sunbeam on thy knees to rest,
And touch those idle hands that folded lie,
Having from sport and toil a like immunity.

Through thy life's dream with what a touching grace
  Childhood attends thee, nearly woman grown;
Her dimples linger yet upon thy face,
  Like dews upon a lily this day blown;
Thy sighs are born of peace, unruffled, deep;
So the babe sighs on mother's breast asleep.

It sighs, and wakes, — but thou! thy dream is all,
  And thou wert born for it, and it for thee;
Morn doth not take thy heart, nor evenfall
  Charm out its sorrowful fidelity,
Nor noon beguile thee from the pastoral shore,
And thy long watch beneath the sycamore.

No, down the Mere as far as eye can see,
  Where its long reaches fade into the sky,
Thy constant gaze, fair child, rests lovingly;
  But neither thou nor any can descry
Aught but the grassy banks, the rustling sedge,
And flocks of wild-fowl splashing at their edge.

And yet 'tis not with expectation hushed
  That thy mute rosy mouth doth pouting close;
No fluttering hope to thy young heart e'er rushed,
  Nor disappointment troubled its repose;
All satisfied with gazing evermore
Along the sunny Mere and reedy shore.

The brooding wren flies pertly near thy seat,
  Thou wilt not move to mark her glancing wing;
The timid sheep browse close before thy feet,
  And heedless at thy side do thrushes sing.
So long amongst them thou hast spent thy days,
They know that harmless hand thou wilt not raise.

Thou wilt not lift it up — not e'en to take
  The foxglove bells that flourish in the shade,
And put them in thy bosom; not to make
  A posy of wild hyacinth inlaid
Like bright mosaic in the mossy grass,
With freckled orchis and pale sassafras.

Gaze on ; — take in the voices of the Mere,
  The break of shallow water at thy feet,
Its plash among long weeds and grasses sere,
  And its weird sobbing, — hollow music meet
For ears like thine ; listen and take thy fill,
And dream on it by night, when all is still.

Full sixteen years have slowly passed away,
  Young Margaret, since thy fond mother here
Came down, a six months' wife, one April day,
  To see her husband's boat go down the Mere,
And track its course, till, lost in distance blue,
In mellow light it faded from her view.

It faded, and she never saw it more ; —
  Nor any human eye ; — oh, grief! oh, woe !
It faded, — and returned not to the shore ;
  But far above it still the waters flow —
And none beheld it sink, and none could tell
Where coldly slept the form she loved so well !

But that sad day, unknowing of her fate,
  She homeward turn'd her still reluctant feet;
And at her wheel she spun, till dark and late,
  The evening fell; — the time when they should meet; —
Till the stars paled that at deep midnight burned —
And morning dawned, and he was not returned.

And the bright sun came up — she thought too soon,
  And shed his ruddy light along the Mere;
And day wore on too quickly, and at noon
  She came and wept beside the waters clear.
"How could he be so late?" — and then hope fled;
And disappointment darkened into dread.

He NEVER came, and she with weepings sore
  Peered in the water-flags unceasingly;
Through all the undulations of the shore,
  Looking for that which most she feared to see.
And then she took home sorrow to her heart,
And brooded over its cold cruel smart.

And after, desolate she sat alone
  And mourned, refusing to be comforted,
On the gray stone, the moss-embroidered stone,
  With the great sycamore above her head;
Till after many days a broken oar
Hard by her seat was drifted to the shore.

It came, — a token of his fate, — the whole,
  The sum of her misfortune to reveal;
As if sent up in pity to her soul,
  The tidings of her widowhood to seal;
And put away the pining hope forlorn,
That made her grief more bitter to be borne.

And she was patient; through the weary day
  She toiled; though none was there her work to bless,
And did not wear the sullen months away,
  Nor call on death to end her wretchedness,
But lest the grief should overflow her breast,
She toiled as heretofore, and would not rest.

But, her work done, what time the evening star
  Rose over the cool water, then she came
To the gray stone, and saw its light from far
  Drop down the misty Mere white lengths of flame,
And wondered whether there might be the place
Where the soft ripple wandered o'er HIS face.

Unfortunate! In solitude forlorn
  She dwelt, and thought upon her husband's grave,
Till when the days grew short a child was born
  To the dead father underneath the wave;
And it brought back a remnant of delight,
A little sunshine to its mother's sight;

A little wonder to her heart grown numb,
  And a sweet yearning pitiful and keen:
She took it as from that poor father come,
  Her and the misery to stand between;
Her little maiden babe, who day by day
Sucked at her breast and charmed her woes away.

But years flew on; the child was still the same,
  Nor human language she had learned to speak;
Her lips were mute, and seasons went and came,
  And brought fresh beauty to her tender cheek;
And all the day upon the sunny shore
She sat and mused beneath the sycamore.

Strange sympathy! she watched and wearied not,
  Haply unconscious what it was she sought;
Her mother's tale she easily forgot,
  And if she listened no warm tears it brought;
Though surely in the yearnings of her heart
The unknown voyager must have had his part.

Unknown to her; like all she saw unknown,
  All sights were fresh as when they first began,
All sounds were new; each murmur and each tone
  And cause and consequence she could not scan,
Forgot that night brought darkness in its train,
Nor reasoned that the day would come again.

There is a happiness in past regret;
  And echoes of the harshest sound are sweet.
The mother's soul was struck with grief, and yet,
  Repeated in her child, 'twas not unmeet
That echo-like the grief a tone should take
Painless, but ever pensive for her sake.

For her dear sake, whose patient soul was linked
  By ties so many to the babe unborn;
Whose hope, by slow degrees become extinct,
  For evermore had left her child forlorn,
Yet left no consciousness of want or woe,
Nor wonder vague that these things should be so.

Truly her joys were limited and few,
  But they sufficed a life to satisfy,
That neither fret nor dim foreboding knew,
  But breathed the air in a great harmony
With its own place and part, and was at one
With all it knew of earth and moon and sun.

For all of them were worked into the dream,
  The husky sighs of wheat-fields in it wrought;
All the land-miles belonged to it; the stream
  That fed the Mere ran through it like a thought.
It was a passion of peace, and loved to wait
'Neath boughs with fair green light illuminate.

To wait with her alone; always alone:
  For any that drew near she heeded not,
Wanting them little as the lily grown
  Apart from others in a shady plot,
Wants fellow-lilies of like fair degree,
In her still glen to bear her company.

Always alone: and yet, there was a child
  Who loved this child, and, from his turret towers,
Across the lea would roam to where, inisled
  And fenced in rapturous silence, went her hours,
And, with slow footsteps drawn anear the place
Where mute she sat, would ponder on her face,

And wonder at her with a childish awe,
And come again to look, and yet again,
Till the sweet rippling of the Mere would draw
His longing to itself; while in her train
The water-hen, come forth, would bring her brood
From slumbering in the rushy solitude;

Or to their young would curlews call and clang
Their homeless young that down the furrows creep;
Or the wind-hover in the blue would hang,
Still as a rock set in the watery deep.
Then from her presence he would break away,
Unmarked, ungreeted yet, from day to day.

But older grown, the Mere he haunted yet,
And a strange joy from its sweet wildness caught;
Whilst careless sat alone maid Margaret,
And "shut the gates" of silence on her thought,
All through spring mornings gemmed with melted rime,
All through hay-harvest and through gleaning time.

O pleasure for itself that boyhood makes,
  O happiness to roam the sighing shore,
Plough up with elfin craft the water-flakes,
  And track the nested rail with cautious oar;
Then floating lie and look with wonder new
Straight up in the great dome of light and blue.

O pleasure! yet they took him from the wold,
  The reedy Mere, and all his pastime there,
The place where he was born, and would grow old
  If God his life so many years should spare;
From the loved haunts of childhood and the plain
And pasture-lands of his own broad domain.

And he came down when wheat was in the sheaf,
  And with her fruit the apple-branch bent low,
While yet in August glory hung the leaf,
  And flowerless aftermath began to grow;
He came from his gray turrets to the shore,
And sought the maid beneath the sycamore.

He sought her, not because her tender eyes
  Would brighten at his coming, for he knew
Full seldom any thought of him would rise
  In her fair breast when he had passed from view;
But for his own love's sake, that unbeguiled
Drew him in spirit to the silent child.

For boyhood in its better hour is prone
  To reverence what it hath not understood;
And he had thought some heavenly meaning shone
  From her clear eyes, that made their watchings good;
While a great peacefulness of shade was shed
Like oil of consecration on her head.

A fishing wallet from his shoulder slung,
  With bounding foot he reached the mossy place,
A little moment gently o'er her hung,
  Put back her hair and looked upon her face,
Then fain from that deep dream to wake her yet,
He "Margaret!" low murmured, "Margaret!

A fishing wallet from his shoulder slung,
With bounding foot he reached the mossy place,
A little moment gently o'er her hung,
Put back her hair and looked upon her face.

"Look at me once before I leave the land,
  For I am going, — going, Margaret."
And then she sighed, and, lifting up her hand,
  Laid it along his young fresh cheek, and set
Upon his face those blue twin-deeps, her eyes,
And moved it back from her in troubled wise,

Because he came between her and her fate,
  The Mere. She sighed again as one oppressed;
The waters, shining clear, with delicate
  Reflections wavered on her blameless breast;
And through the branches dropt, like flickerings fair,
And played upon her hands and on her hair.

And he, withdrawn a little space to see,
  Murmured in tender ruth that was not pain,
"Farewell, I go; but sometimes think of me,
  Maid Margaret;" and there came by again
A whispering in the reed-beds and the sway
Of waters: then he turned and went his way.

And wilt thou think on him now he is gone?
  No; thou wilt gaze: though thy young eyes grow dim,
And thy soft cheek become all pale and wan,
  Still thou wilt gaze, and spend no thought on him;
There is no sweetness in his laugh for thee—
No beauty in his fresh heart's gayety.

But wherefore linger in deserted haunts?
  Why of the past, as if yet present, sing?
The yellow iris on the margin flaunts,
  With hyacinth the banks are blue in spring,
And under dappled clouds the lark afloat
Pours all the April-tide from her sweet throat.

But Margaret—ah! thou art there no more,
  And thick dank moss creeps over thy gray stone;
Thy path is lost that skirted the low shore,
  With willow-grass and speedwell overgrown;
Thine eye has closed for ever, and thine ear
Drinks in no more the music of the Mere.

The boy shall come — shall come again in spring,
  Well pleased that pastoral solitude to share,
And some kind offering in his hand will bring
  To cast into thy lap, O maid most fair —
Some clasping gem about thy neck to rest,
Or heave and glimmer on thy guileless breast.

And he shall wonder why thou art not here
  The solitude with "smiles to entertain,"
And gaze along the reaches of the Mere;
  But he shall never see thy face again —
Shall never see upon the reedy shore
Maid Margaret beneath her sycamore.

II.

MARGARET IN THE XEBEC.

["Concerning this man (Robert Delacour), little further is known than tha he served in the king's army, and was wounded in the battle of Marston Moor being then about twenty-seven years of age. After the battle of Nazeby, finding himself a marked man, he quitted the country, taking with him the chil whom he had adopted; and he made many voyages between the different port of the Mediterranean and Levant."]

RESTING within his tent at turn of day,
A wailing voice his scanty sleep beset:
He started up — it did not flee away —
'Twas no part of his dream, but still did fret
And pine into his heart, "Ah me! ah me!"
Broken with heaving sobs right mournfully.

Then he arose, and, troubled at this thing,
  All wearily toward the voice he went
Over the down-trod bracken and the ling,
  Until it brought him to a soldier's tent,
Where, with the tears upon her face, he found
A little maiden weeping on the ground;

And backward in the tent an aged crone
  Upbraided her full harshly more and more,
But sunk her chiding to an undertone
  When she beheld him standing at the door,
And calmed her voice, and dropped her lifted hand,
And answered him with accent soft and bland.

No, the young child was none of hers, she said,
  But she had found her where the ash lay white
About a smouldering tent; her infant head
  All shelterless, she through the dewy night
Had slumbered on the field, — ungentle fate
For a lone child so soft and delicate.

"And I," quoth she, "have tended her with care,
  And thought to be rewarded of her kin,
For by her rich attire and features fair
  I know her birth is gentle: yet within
The tent unclaimed she doth but pine and weep,
A burden I would fain no longer keep."

Still while she spoke the little creature wept,
  Till painful pity touched him for the flow
Of all those tears, and to his heart there crept
  A yearning as of fatherhood, and lo!
Reaching his arms to her, "My sweet," quoth he,
"Dear little madam, wilt thou come with me?"

Then she left off her crying, and a look
  Of wistful wonder stole into her eyes.
The sullen frown her dimpled face forsook,
  She let him take her, and forgot her sighs,
Contented in his alien arms to rest,
And lay her baby head upon his breast.

Ah, sure a stranger trust was never sought
  By any soldier on a battle-plain.
He brought her to his tent, and soothed his voice,
  Rough with command; and asked, but all in vain,
Her story, while her prattling tongue rang sweet,
She playing, as one at home, about his feet.

Of race, of country, or of parentage,
  Her lisping accents nothing could unfold; —
No questioning could win to read the page
  Of her short life; — she left her tale untold,
And home and kin thus early to forget,
She only knew, — her name was — Margaret.

Then in the dusk upon his arm it chanced
  That night that suddenly she fell asleep;
And he looked down on her like one entranced,
  And listened to her breathing still and deep,
As if a little child, when daylight closed,
With half-shut lids had ne'er before reposed.

Softly he laid her down from off his arm,
With earnest care and new-born tenderness:
Her infancy, a wonder-working charm,
Laid hold upon his love; he stayed to bless
The small sweet head, then went he forth that night
And sought a nurse to tend this new delight.

And day by day his heart she wrought upon,
And won her way into its inmost fold—
A heart which, but for lack of that whereon
To fix itself, would never have been cold;
And, opening wide, now let her come to dwell
Within its strong unguarded citadel.

She, like a dream, unlocked the hidden springs
Of his past thoughts, and set their current free
To talk with him of half-forgotten things—
The pureness and the peace of infancy,
"Thou also, thou," to sigh, "wert undefiled
(O God, the change!) once, as this little child."

The baby-mistress of a soldier's heart,
  She had but friendlessness to stand her friend,
And her own orphanhood to plead her part,
  When he, a wayfarer, did pause, and bend,
And bear with him the starry blossom sweet
Out of its jeopardy from trampling feet.

A gleam of light upon a rainy day,
  A new-tied knot that must be sever'd soon,
At sunrise once before his tent at play,
  And hurried from the battle-field at noon,
While face to face in hostile ranks they stood,
Who should have dwelt in peace and brotherhood.

But ere the fight, when higher rose the sun,
  And yet were distant far the rebel bands,
She heard at intervals a booming gun,
  And she was pleased, and laughing clapped her hands;
Till he came in with troubled look and tone,
Who chose her desolate to be his own.

And he said, "Little madam, now farewell,
  For there will be a battle fought ere night.
God be thy shield, for He alone can tell
  Which way may fall the fortune of the fight.
To fitter hands the care of thee pertain,
My dear, if we two never meet again."

Then he gave money shortly to her nurse,
  And charged her straitly to depart in haste,
And leave the plain, whereon the deadly curse
  Of war should light with ruin, death, and waste,
And all the ills that must its presence blight,
E'en if proud victory should bless the right.

"But if the rebel cause should prosper, then
  It were not good among the hills to wend;
But journey through to Boston in the fen,
  And wait for peace, if peace our God shall send;
And if my life is spared, I will essay,"
Quoth he, "to join you there as best I may."

So then he kissed the child, and went his way;
  But many troubles rolled above his head;
The sun arose on many an evil day,
  And cruel deeds were done, and tears were shed;
And hope was lost, and loyal hearts were fain
In dust to hide, — ere they two met again.

So passed the little child from thought, from view —
  (The snowdrop blossoms, and then is not there,
Forgotten till men welcome it anew),
  He found her in his heavy days of care,
And with her dimples was again beguiled,
As on her nurse's knee she sat and smiled.

And he became a voyager by sea,
  And took the child to share his wandering state;
Since from his native land compelled to flee,
  And hopeless to avert her monarch's fate;
For all was lost that might have made him pause,
And, past a soldier's help, the royal cause.

And thus rolled on long days, long months and years,
  And Margaret within the Xebec sailed;
The lulling wind made music in her ears,
  And nothing to her life's completeness failed.
Her pastime 'twas to see the dolphins spring,
And wonderful live rainbows glimmering.

The gay sea-plants familiar were to her,
  As daisies to the children of the land;
Red wavy dulse the sunburnt mariner
  Raised from its bed to glisten in her hand;
The vessel and the sea were her life's stage—
Her house, her garden, and her hermitage.

Also she had a cabin of her own,
  For beauty like an elfin palace bright,
With Venice glass adorned and crystal stone,
  That trembled with a many-colored light;
And there with two caged ringdoves she did play,
And feed them carefully from day to day.

Her bed with silken curtains was enclosed,
  White as the snowy rose of Guelderland;
On Turkish pillows her young head reposed,
  And love had gathered with a careful hand
Fair playthings to the little maiden's side,
From distant ports, and cities parted wide.

She had two myrtle-plants that she did tend,
  And think all trees were like to them that grew:
For things on land she did confuse and blend,
  And chiefly from the deck the land she knew,
And in her heart she pitied more and more
The steadfast dwellers on the changeless shore.

Green fields and inland meadows faded out
  Of mind, or with sea images were linked;
And yet she had her childish thoughts about
  The country she had left — though indistinct
And faint as mist the mountain-head that shrouds,
Or dim through distance as Magellan's clouds.

And when to frame a forest scene she tried,
  The ever-present sea would yet intrude,
And all her towns were by the water's side,
  It murmured in all moorland solitude,
Where rocks and the ribbed sand would intervene,
And waves would edge her fancied village green;

Because her heart was like an ocean shell,
  That holds (men say) a message from the deep;
And yet the land was strong, she knew its spell,
  And harbor lights could draw her in her sleep;
And minster chimes from piercèd towers that swim,
Were the land-angels making God a hymn.

So she grew on, the idol of one heart,
  And the delight of many — and her face,
Thus dwelling chiefly from her sex apart,
  Was touched with a most deep and tender grace —
A look that never aught but nature gave,
Artless, yet thoughtful; innocent, yet grave.

Strange her adornings were, and strangely blent:
  A golden net confined her nut-brown hair;
Quaint were the robes that divers lands had lent,
  And quaint her aged nurse's skill and care;
Yet did they well on the sea-maiden meet,
Circle her neck, and grace her dimpled feet.

The sailor folk were glad because of her,
  And deemed good fortune followed in her wake;
She was their guardian saint, they did aver —
  Prosperous winds were sent them for her sake;
And strange rough vows, strange prayers, they nightly made,
While, storm or calm, she slept, in nought afraid.

Clear were her eyes, that daughter of the sea,
  Sweet, when uplifted to her aged nurse,
She sat, and communed what the world could be;
  And rambling stories caused her to rehearse
How Yule was kept, how maidens tossed the hay,
And how bells rang upon a wedding day.

But they grew brighter when the evening star
  First trembled over the still glowing wave,
That bathed in ruddy light, mast, sail, and spar;
  For then, reclined in rest that twilight gave,
With him who served for father, friend, and guide,
She sat upon the deck at eventide.

Then turned towards the west, that on her hair
  And her young cheek shed down its tender glow,
He taught her many things with earnest care
  That he thought fitting a young maid should know,
Told of the good deeds of the worthy dead,
And prayers devout, by faithful martyrs said.

And many psalms he caused her to repeat
  And sing them, at his knees reclined the while,
And spoke with her of all things good and meet,
  And told the story of her native isle,
Till at the end he made her tears to flow,
Rehearsing of his royal master's woe.

And of the stars he taught her, and their names,
  And how the chartless mariner they guide;
Of quivering light that in the zenith flames,
  Of monsters in the deep sea caves that hide;
Then changed the theme to fairy records wild,
Enchanted moor, elf dame, or changeling child.

To her the Eastern lands their strangeness spread,
  The dark-faced Arab in his long blue gown,
The camel thrusting down a snake-like head
  To browse on thorns outside a walled white town,
Where palmy clusters rank by rank upright
Float as in quivering lakes of ribbèd light.

And when the ship sat like a broad-winged bird
  Becalmed, lo, lions answered in the night
Their fellows, all the hollow dark was stirred
  To echo on that tremulous thunder's flight,
Dying in weird faint moans; — till look! the sun
And night, and all the things of night, were done.

And they, toward the waste as morning brake,
Turned, where, inisled in his green watered land,
The Lybian Zeus lay couched of old, and spake,
Hemmed in with leagues of furrow-facèd sand —
Then saw the moon (like Joseph's golden cup
Come back) behind some ruined roof swim up.

But blooming childhood will not always last,
And storms will rise e'en on the tideless sea;
His guardian love took fright, she grew so fast,
And he began to think how sad 'twould be
If he should die, and pirate hordes should get
By sword or shipwreck his fair Margaret.

It was a sudden thought; but he gave way,
For it assailed him with unwonted force;
And, with no more than one short week's delay,
For English shores he shaped the vessel's course;
And ten years absent saw her landed now,
With thirteen summers on her maiden brow.

And so he journeyed with her, far inland,
  Down quiet lanes, by hedges gemmed with dew,
Where wonders met her eye on every hand,
  And all was beautiful and strange and new —
All, from the forest trees in stately ranks,
To yellow cowslips trembling on the banks.

All new — the long-drawn slope of evening shades,
  The sweet solemnities of waxing light,
The white-haired boys, the blushing rustic maids,
  The ruddy gleam through cottage casements bright,
The green of pastures, bloom of garden nooks,
And endless bubbling of the water-brooks.

So far he took them on through this green land,
  The maiden and her nurse, till journeying
They saw at last a peaceful city stand
  On a steep mount, and heard its clear bells ring.
High were the towers and rich with ancient state,
In its old wall enclosed and massive gate.

There dwelt a worthy matron whom he knew,
  To whom in time of war he gave good aid,
Shielding her household from the plundering crew
  When neither law could bind nor worth persuade:
And to her house he brought his care and pride,
Aweary with the way and sleepy-eyed.

And he, the man whom she was fain to serve,
  Delayed not shortly his request to make,
Which was, if aught of her he did deserve,
  To take the maid, and rear her for his sake,
To guard her youth, and let her breeding be
In womanly reserve and modesty.

And that same night into the house he brought
  The costly fruits of all his voyages —
Rich Indian gems of wandering craftsmen wrought,
  Long ropes of pearls from Persian palaces,
With ingots pure and coins of Venice mould,
And silver bars and bags of Spanish gold;

And costly merchandise of far-off lands,
  And golden stuffs and shawls of Eastern dye,
He gave them over to the matron's hands,
  With jewelled gauds, and toys of ivory,
To be her dower on whom his love was set, —
His dearest child, fair Madam Margaret.

Then he entreated, that if he should die,
  She would not cease her guardian mission mild.
Awhile, as undecided, lingered nigh,
  Beside the pillow of the sleeping child,
Severed one wandering lock of wavy hair,
Took horse that night, and left her unaware.

And it was long before he came again —
  So long that Margaret was woman grown;
And oft she wished for his return in vain,
  Calling him softly in an undertone;
Repeating words that he had said the while,
And striving to recall his look and smile.

If she had known — oh, if she could have known —
The toils, the hardships of those absent years —
How bitter thraldom forced the unwilling groan —
How slavery wrung out subduing tears,
Not calmly had she passed her hours away,
Chiding half pettishly the long delay.

But she was spared. She knew no sense of harm,
While the red flames ascended from the deck;
Saw not the pirate band the crew disarm,
Mourned not the floating spars, the smoking wreck.
She did not dream, and there was none to tell,
That fetters bound the hands she ioved so well.

Sweet Margaret — withdrawn from human view,
She spent long hours beneath the cedar shade,
The stately trees that in the garden grew,
And, overtwined, a towering shelter made;
She mused among the flowers, and birds, and bees,
In winding walks, and bowering canopies;

Or wandered slowly through the ancient rooms,
  Where oriel windows shed their rainbow gleams;
And tapestried hangings, wrought in Flemish looms,
  Displayed the story of King Pharaoh's dreams;
And, come at noon because the well was deep,
Beautiful Rachel leading down her sheep.

At last she reached the bloom of womanhood,
  After five summers spent in growing fair;
Her face betokened all things dear and good,
  The light of somewhat yet to come was there
Asleep, and waiting for the opening day,
When childish thoughts, like flowers, would drift away.

O! we are far too happy while they last;
  We have our good things first, and they cost naught;
Then the new splendor comes unfathomed, vast,
  A costly trouble, ay, a sumptuous thought,
And will not wait, and cannot be possessed,
Though infinite yearnings fold it to the breast.

And time, that seemed so long, is fleeting by,
  And life is more than life ; love more than love ;
We have not found the whole — and we must die —
  And still the unclasped glory floats above.
The inmost and the utmost faint from sight,
For ever secret in their veil of light.

Be not too hasty in your flow, you rhymes,
  For Margaret is in her garden bower ;
Delay to ring, you soft cathedral chimes,
  And tell not out too soon the noontide hour :
For one draws nearer to your ancient town,
On the green mount down settled like a crown.

He journeyed on, and, as he neared the gate,
  He met with one to whom he named the maid,
Inquiring of her welfare, and her state,
  And of the matron in whose house she stayed.
"The maiden dwelt there yet," the townsman said ;
"But, for the ancient lady, — she was dead."

He further said, she was but little known,
  Although reputed to be very fair,
And little seen (so much she dwelt alone)
  But with her nurse at stated morning prayer;
So seldom passed her sheltering garden wall,
Or left the gate at quiet evening fall.

Flow softly, rhymes — his hand is on the door;
  Ring out, ye noonday bells, his welcoming —
"He went out rich, but he returneth poor;"
  And strong — now something bowed with suffering.
And on his brow are traced long furrowed lines,
Earned in the fight with pirate Algerines.

Her aged nurse comes hobbling at his call;
  Lifts up her withered hand in dull surprise,
And, tottering, leads him through the pillared hall;
  "What! come at last to bless my lady's eyes!
Dear heart, sweet heart, she's grown a likesome maid —
Go, seek her where she sitteth in the shade."

The noonday chime had ceased — she did not know
  Who watched her, while her ringdoves fluttered near;
While, under the green boughs, in accents low
  She sang unto herself. She did not hear
His footstep till she turned, then rose to meet
Her guest with guileless blush and wonder sweet.

But soon she knew him, came with quickened pace,
  And put her gentle hands about his neck;
And leaned her fair cheek to his sun-burned face,
  As long ago upon the vessel's deck:
As long ago she did in twilight deep,
When heaving waters lulled her infant sleep.

So then he kissed her, as men kiss their own,
  And, proudly parting her unbraided hair,
He said: "I did not think to see thee grown
  So fair a woman," — but a touch of care
The deep-toned voice through its caressing kept,
And, hearing it, she turned away and wept.

Wept, — for an impress on the face she viewed —
  The stamp of feelings she remembered not;
His voice was calmer now, but more subdued,
  Not like the voice long loved and unforgot!
She felt strange sorrow and delightful pain —
Grief for the change, joy that he came again.

O pleasant days, that followed his return,
  That made his captive years pass out of mind;
If life had yet new pains for him to learn,
  Not in the maid's clear eyes he saw it shrined;
And three full weeks he stayed with her, content
To find her beautiful and innocent.

It was all one in his contented sight
  As though she were a child, till suddenly,
Waked of the chimes in the dead time of the night,
  He fell to thinking how the urgency
Of Fate had dealt with him, and could but sigh
For those best things wherein she passed him by.

Down the long river of life how, cast adrift,
  She urged him on, still on, to sink or swim;
And all at once, as if a veil did lift,
  In the dead time of the night, and bare to him
The want in his deep soul, he looked, was dumb,
And knew himself, and knew his time was come.

In the dead time of the night his soul did sound
  The dark sea of a trouble unforeseen,
For that one sweet that to his life was bound
  Had turned into a want — a misery keen:
Was born, was grown, and wounded sorely cried
All 'twixt the midnight and the morning tide.

He was a brave man, and he took this thing
  And cast it from him with a man's strong hand;
And that next morn, with no sweet altering
  Of mien, beside the maid he took his stand,
And copied his past self till ebbing day
Paled its deep western blush, and died away.

And then he told her that he must depart
  Upon the morrow, with the earliest light;
And it displeased and pained her at the heart,
  And she went out to hide her from his sight
Aneath the cedar trees, where dusk was deep,
And be apart from him awhile to weep

And to lament, till, suddenly aware
  Of steps, she started up as fain to flee,
And met him in the moonlight pacing there,
  Who questioned with her why her tears might be,
Till she did answer him, all red for shame,
"Kind sir, I weep — the wanting of a name."

"A name!" quoth he, and sighed. "I never knew
  Thy father's name; but many a stalwart youth
Would give thee his, dear child, and his love too,
  And count himself a happy man forsooth.
Is there none here who thy kind thought hath won?"
But she did falter, and made answer, "None."

Then, as in father-like and kindly mood,
  He said, "Dear daughter, it would please me well
To see thee wed; for know it is not good
  That a fair woman thus alone should dwell."
She said, "I am content it should be so,
If when you journey I may with you go."

This when he heard, he thought, right sick at heart.
  Must I withstand myself, and also thee?
Thou, also thou! must nobly do thy part;
  That honor leads thee on which holds back me.
No, thou sweet woman; by love's great increase,
I will reject thee for thy truer peace.

Then said he, "Lady! — look upon my face;
  Consider well this scar upon my brow;
I have had all misfortune but disgrace;
  I do not look for marriage blessings now.
Be not thy gratitude deceived. I know
Thou think'st it is thy duty — I will go!

"I read thy meaning, and I go from hence,
  Skilled in the reason; though my heart be rude,
I will not wrong thy gentle innocence,
  Nor take advantage of thy gratitude.
But think, while yet the light these eyes shall bless,
The more for thee — of woman's nobleness."

Faultless and fair, all in the moony light,
  As one ashamed, she looked upon the ground,
And her white raiment glistened in his sight.
  And, hark! the vesper chimes began to sound,
Then lower yet she drooped her young, pure cheek,
And still was she ashamed, and could not speak.

A swarm of bells from that old tower o'erhead,
  They sent their message sifting through the boughs
Of cedars; when they ceased his lady said,
  "Pray you forgive me," and her lovely brows
She lifted, standing in her moonlit place,
And one short moment looked him in the face.

Then straight he cried, "O sweetheart, think all one
As no word yet were said between us twain,
And know thou that in this I yield to none—
I love thee, sweetheart, love thee!" So full fain,
While she did leave to silence all her part,
He took the gleaming whiteness to his heart—

The white-robed maiden with the warm white throat,
The sweet white brow, and locks of umber flow,
Whose murmuring voice was soft as rock-dove's note,
Entreating him, and saying, "Do not go!"
"I will not, sweetheart; nay, not now," quoth he,
"By faith and troth, I think thou art for me!"

And so she won a name that eventide,
Which he gave gladly, but would ne'er bespeak,
And she became the rough sea-captain's bride,
Matching her dimples to his sunburnt cheek;
And chasing from his voice the touch of care,
That made her weep when first she heard it there.

One year there was, fulfilled of happiness,
  But O! it went so fast, too fast away.
Then came that trouble which full oft doth bless —
  It was the evening of a sultry day,
There was no wind the thread-hung flowers to stir,
Or float abroad the filmy gossamer.

Toward the trees his steps the mariner bent,
  Pacing the grassy walks with restless feet:
And he recalled, and pondered as he went,
  All her most duteous love and converse sweet,
Till summer darkness settled deep and dim,
And dew from bending leaves dropt down on him.

The flowers sent forth their nightly odors faint —
  Thick leaves shut out the starlight overhead;
While he told over, as by strong constraint
  Drawn on, her childish life on shipboard led,
And beauteous youth, since first low kneeling there,
With folded hands she lisped her evening prayer.

Then he remembered how, beneath the shade,
  She wooed him to her with her lovely words,
While flowers were closing, leaves in moonlight played,
  And in dark nooks withdrew the silent birds.
So pondered he that night in twilight dim,
While dew from bending leaves dropt down on him.

The flowers sent forth their nightly odors faint —
  When, in the darkness waiting, he saw one
To whom he said — "How fareth my sweet saint?"
  Who answered — "She hath borne to you a son;"
Then, turning, left him, — and the father said,
"God rain down blessings on his welcome head!"

But Margaret! — *she* never saw the child,
  Nor heard about her bed love's mournful wails;
But to the last, with ocean dreams beguiled,
  Murmured of troubled seas and swelling sails —
Of weary voyages, and rocks unseen,
And distant hills in sight, all calm and green. . . .

Woe and alas! — the times of sorrow come,
  And make us doubt if we were ever glad!
So utterly that inner voice is dumb,
  Whose music through our happy days we had!
So, at the touch of grief, without our will,
The sweet voice drops from us, and all is still.

Woe and alas! for the sea-captain's wife —
  That Margaret who in the Xebec played —
She spent upon his knee her baby life;
  Her slumbering head upon his breast she laid.
How shall he learn alone his years to pass?
How in the empty house? — woe and alas!

She died, and in the aisle, the minster aisle,
  They made her grave; and there, with fond intent,
Her husband raised, his sorrow to beguile,
  A very fair and stately monument:
Her tomb (the careless vergers show it yet),
The mariner's wife, his love, his Margaret.

A woman's figure, with the eyelids closed,
The quiet head declined in slumber sweet;
Upon an anchor one fair hand reposed,
And a long ensign folded at her feet,
And carved upon the bordering of her vest
The motto of her house—"He giveth rest."

There is an ancient window richly fraught
And fretted with all hues most rich, most bright,
And in its upper tracery enwrought
An olive-branch and dove wide-winged and white,
An emblem meet for her, the tender dove,
Her heavenly peace, her duteous earthly love.

Amid heraldic shields and banners set,
In twisted knots and wildly-tangled bands,
Crimson and green, and gold and violet,
Fall softly on the snowy sculptured hands;
And, when the sunshine comes, full sweetly rest
The dove and olive-branch upon her breast.

NEW BOOKS

FOR THE

AUTUMN AND WINTER OF 1870–71.

JEAN INGELOW. THE MONITIONS OF THE UNSEEN, AND OTHER NEW POEMS, including a Christmas Poem called "The Mariner's Cave." The book will be beautifully illustrated, and will be ready Dec. 1.

SYLVESTER JUDD. MARGARET. A Tale of the Real and the Ideal, of Blight and Bloom. 16mo. Price $1.50.

EDWARD E. HALE. TEN TIMES ONE IS TEN. The Possible Reformation. A Story. 16mo. Price $1.25.

HARRIET W. PRESTON. ASPENDALE: A STORY AND AN ESSAY. 16mo. Price $1.50.

ARTHUR HELPS. ESSAYS WRITTEN IN THE INTERVALS OF BUSINESS. To which is added "Organization in Daily Life." 16mo. Price $1.50.

ARTHUR HELPS. SHORT ESSAYS AND APHORISMS. 16mo.

WALTER SAVAGE LANDOR. PERICLES AND ASPASIA. 16mo. Price $1.50.

J. R. SEELEY. (Author of "Ecce Homo.") ROMAN IMPERIALISM, and other Papers. 16mo. Price $1.50

J. R. SEELEY. LECTURES ON ROMAN HISTORY. 16mo.

PAUL KONEWKA. SILHOUETTE ILLUSTRATIONS TO GOETHE'S FAUST, with English text from Bayard Taylor's new Translation. One elegant quarto. Price $4.00.

JOHN WHOPPER'S ADVENTURES. With Illustrations.

Published by ROBERTS BROTHERS,
BOSTON.

www.ingramcontent.com/pod-product-compliance
Lightning Source LLC
LaVergne TN
LVHW011216110826
845150LV00006B/1439

9781425517083